YOU'RE A VAMPIRE

— THAT SUCKS! —

A SURVIVAL GUIDE

"Count" Domenick Dicce

JEREMY P. TARCHER/PENGUIN   A MEMBER OF PENGUIN RANDOM HOUSE   NEW YORK

JEREMY P. TARCHER/PENGUIN
An imprint of Penguin Random House LLC
375 Hudson Street
New York, New York 10014

Illustrations © 2015 by Rick Shiers

Library of Congress Cataloging-in-Publication Data
Dicce, Domenick.
You're a vampire—that sucks! : a survival guide / by
"Count" Domenick Dicce.
pages cm
ISBN 978-0-399-17588-6 (paperback)
1. Vampires—Humor.   I. Title.
PN6231.V27D53   2015   2015016533
818'.602—dc23

Book design by Meighan Cavanaugh

149062918

Praise for
You're a Vampire—That Sucks!

"A must-read for the recently dead, which walks the reader through the first and awkward years of vampirism. This Transylvanian romp will have you giggling as it guides you through finding a decent meal, making fang-toothed friends, and avoiding wooden-stake-wielding psychopaths."

—TAYLOR BAYOUTH, AUTHOR OF *How to Steal the Mona Lisa*

"*You're a Vampire—That Sucks!* is prescribed for treatment of moderate to severe cases of nosferatu ennui. Side effects include laughter and prolonged snickering. Warning: reading Domenick Dicce may become habit-forming."

—E. E. KNIGHT, AUTHOR OF THE VAMPIRE EARTH SERIES

"Finally, a guide for the living undead! Count Dicce's delightful book helps the novice vampire deal with everything from finding a suitable job to recipe tips for creatively satisfying your insatiable blood lust. A fun, informative guide that I know I'll be relying on."

—ANDREW MAYNE, AUTHOR OF *Angel Killer*

YOU'RE A VAMPIRE—

THAT SUCKS!

CONTENTS

YOU'RE A
VAMPIRE—

THAT
SUCKS!

— I —

Welcome: Velcome

S o, you're a vampire. That sucks! Transforming from a human to a vampire can be quite traumatic—one minute, you're craving a slice of pizza, the next, you're craving a slice of somebody's bleeding finger. Sadly, due to the solitary nature of us vampires, chances are you're reading this book because the bloodsucker that turned you has already come and gone. Wham, bam, suck you, ma'am! It's just like the undead to leave you outside like a piece of roadkill. While not all vampires are ghastly, generally we are not the warmest of creatures.

Having been through this experience myself, I wanted to help others. This transition will be one of the biggest moments in your undead life, and nothing is harder than the first year. Most vampires are killed within this time. My only hope is that this book makes your transition smoother and safer than mine was. The knowledge I share could be the difference between an eternity of happiness and a lifetime brooding alone in misery until you become an untimely pile of dust blowing away in the wind.

By opening this book, you have already taken your first step in coming to terms not only with who you are, but what you are capable of. Most vampires go about this journey the wrong way. Usually they use trial and error, often accompanied by brushes with actual death or angry torch-carrying mobs—both undesirable. Some try to find older vampires to be their mentor—bad idea. We generally hide out for a reason: safety! Vampires do not take kindly to newbies bringing them out of concealment and possibly making them the next guest at a stake-throwing party. The truly naïve do their research through vampire lore—rookie mistake. Although some facts are found this way, there are many more myths, half-truths, and downright lies. We vampires have spread most of these falsehoods ourselves, in order to help with our survival. Do you really think vampires can't come into your home if you don't invite them? If that were true, I'd have missed out on a lot of good meals!

I know this new world is confusing and the transition is difficult, but I am determined to save you the pain and humiliation I experienced. I only wish this kind of book had been around a few hundred years ago—it might have saved me a lot of grief. Read on, and we'll get you through this together. Remember to always keep this book in a safe place. We can only survive if people think we are imaginary and non-threatening.

Oh, and if you're a human and still reading this book? Fooled you! Aren't vampire tales hilarious? Ha ha ha . . . um . . . I am always up for meeting a fan. Let's talk over dinner soon!

II

Feeding: Got Blood?

First of all, let's get one thing straight: We are not carnivores. We are sanguinivores. Sanguinivores feed on the blood of vertebrates. This is the only time I will use really big words to show off how smart I am. It comes with being around for a few hundred years. Simply put, we do not eat meat. We drink the blood of animals with a backbone or spine—the fresher the source, the tastier and more nutritious the blood. Like all-natural food, blood spoils. Luckily this is rather easy to tell since blood is good to eat in its liquid form. Once blood dries, it loses all nutritional value, though rest assured it takes more than rancid blood to kill a vampire!

We are not limited to a strictly human diet, although human blood is the most nutritious. It allows you to grow stronger and quickly recover from any injuries suffered due to a recent fight or an overestimation of capabilities. We vampires do tend to be excessively confident in our abilities—maybe we should drop the whole "immortal" mentality. Human blood is unique in both its taste and nutritional factors. Not only will it be the most amazing flavor you have ever encountered, but your whole body will fill with what I can only describe as pure energy. In the vampire world we have a saying: Once you've had a human snack, you never go back.

If the thought of drinking human blood makes you a little squeamish, then you can live on an animal diet. This, however, is not recommended. You'll never grow as strong as human-eaters and your appetite will never truly be satisfied. But hey, even vampires deserve free will. You don't need to be ashamed of abstaining from humans in the beginning. This is completely normal and nothing to be embarrassed of. The older vampires will tease you about your zoogan eating habit, but they've probably secretly tried it themselves. It's not an easy diet to stick with.

VAMPIRE FOOD PYRAMID

If you are still a stiff about not drinking blood as the years go on, then try to eat as genotypically close to humans as possible. Of course the closest animals to humans are gorillas, chimpanzees, and other primates, but you probably won't want to break into your local zoo to feed. Unless you live in an African jungle, my advice is to find another source. Most mammals will do a decent job of sustaining you, but I have found rats are the most reliable. Their DNA is remarkably similar to humans, which is why humans use them for so many of their medical experiments. The nice thing about vermin is that they are everywhere, and people never miss them. If you eat someone's dog, Fluffy, chances are there will be a very upset owner looking for the lost pet. The only downside with rats is that they are small and don't fill you up. Well, unless you are hunting in a New York subway. Those things get huge!

Not into rats? Okay, we'll find you something else, but don't go back to beef. You may have eaten it in your other life, but you bought it. Killing a farmer's source of income will more often than not lead to an investigation. For this reason you should probably avoid all livestock. Sure, it's filling, but it's not worth the risk. Besides, do you really need to drain an entire cow? Let's not be gluttons here. Even though you do not gain weight, there is no reason to overindulge.

Nutritionally speaking, birds are the next best things for you. But logistically speaking, they are the most difficult and time consuming to catch. The whole flight thing makes them tricky prey, and then when you do get ahold of them, the feathers make it very uncomfortable to enjoy. You could pluck them, but this takes forever and then you have to deal with feathers being all over the place. They are just a pain in the fang.

Fish are also excellent sources of blood, but again, difficult to catch. I enjoy eating them more than birds, though some find their slimy texture a little hard to handle. The upside is, if you like to fish, they tend to bite when the sun has set. This is a plus, considering the sun will kill you (more on this later—in the meantime, stay out of the sun). Make sure to check local laws about what times you are allowed to fish along with what is in season. We're vampires, not criminals! Yes, a person dying might be the by-product of us feeding, but the definition of murder is "the unlawful killing of one human being by another," and we are not human. I would not use this defense in court, but it should help your conscience as you transition away from your human past.

Reptiles are next on your list of nutritional food

choices. They are plentiful and tend to be easier to catch than birds and fish. You can live off reptiles indefinitely, but again, you will not be a strong, healthy vampire. Because reptiles are cold-blooded, they are the junk food of the animal kingdom. They taste delicious but offer little nutritional value. You're probably wondering why cold-blooded fish are so healthy. I theorize it has something to do with being leftover from our human lives where we ate fish more often or some other biological reason, but I have no idea. After all, I am a vampire, not a biologist.

Last on our list of drinkable blood are amphibians. Although just as nutritious as reptiles, they are my least favorite creatures to suck on. Before you even ask, NO, sucking on a toad will not give you warts.

The problem with amphibians is that you take one bite into them and you have a disgusting slimy coating on your tongue for the next hour. If you absolutely must eat amphibians, I would suggest using your fingernails to slice open a major vein and just squeezing the blood out of them. This is highly inefficient, but much more pleasant than a slimy tongue.

BAD BLOOD

You cannot eat bugs to sustain yourself. This myth was started because of the character Renfield in Bram Stoker's *Dracula*. The idea behind this is that vampires consume blood for the "life-force" it contains. Life-force is this concept of spiritual energy in living creatures. This life-force can be absorbed to a lesser extent by consuming living creatures such as insects. Eating bugs is just plain disgusting and, to me, insane. I am not alone in believing Renfield would have been crazy for doing this. In the medical profession, Renfield has his own diagnosis. It is referred to as Renfield's syndrome, which is a rare psychiatric disorder in which the sufferer feels a compulsion to consume blood. According to current psychiatric terminology, Renfield's syndrome is classified as schizophrenia or paraphilia. These people who believe they are vampires have been a blessing and a curse. On one hand, they are

easy scapegoats for us to blame if we should accidentally reveal ourselves. On the other hand, they just
give vampires a bad name.

Until some mad scientists come up with a syn-
thetic blood for us all to drink, we don't have other
options. This is as good a time as any to start getting
rid of some myths about our eating habits. While
most of these items will just make you really sick,
there are a few lethal ones you should stay clear of.

Eating solid food will not kill you. Unless you are
stupid enough to eat garlic, in which case, according
to Darwin, you should not exist anyway. Thanks for
weeding yourself out. If you attempt to eat any solid
food, you will go through two stages. The first is wor-
rying that you are going to die, and the second stage is
wishing you would die. In human terms, it is a very
bad case of food poisoning. Sadly, yes, you are not
going to know which end of your body to position
over the toilet first. This may in turn lead to some
very awkward moments. This will be the only time in
which a vampire will have a bowel movement. (Ladies, you will be happy to know that your butt is now
really only for decoration. Since we now subsist on an
all-blood diet, using the restroom is a thing of the
past—we absorb the blood into our system.)

If you try to drink any liquid besides blood, you
will instantly puke it back up. Fortunately this is a

rather painless process, and you will experience no discomfort as you vomit. Films love showing vampires sipping red wine instead of blood, but watching a real vampire hurl red wine immediately after swallowing it takes away any semblance of elegance. However, there is an exception: You can mix your favorite beverage with blood to enjoy a hint of that original taste from your living days once again. The ratio must be 90 percent blood to 10 percent liquid. Any more non-blood liquid than 10 percent and you will spew. Our sense of taste is also greatly enhanced, so even this small percent will be very apparent to you. As you grow older, you will crave these old flavors less and less, but the craving will never entirely go away. After all these years, I still enjoy a little coffee mixed in with my blood.

It is recommended that you do not feed from vampires, werewolves, or other supernatural creatures. A drop won't do much, but any more than that is a gamble. Supernatural blood is the equivalent of doing drugs for vampires. This could kill you or, at the very least, lead to a temporary psychological breakdown. The effects depend on which creature you drink, how powerful they are, and how much you consume. The pure energy mentioned earlier when consuming human blood is magnified a hundred times. Your body is filled with so much of this raw energy that it cannot be contained. You will be reduced to a raging beast with all your powers at full strength going off at once, while your mental reasoning is severely impaired. There is always a vampire who thinks they can control it if they just drink a little. This is a mistake. Friends don't let friends drink supernatural blood.

FEEDING MYTHS

We also don't feed off a person's life-force or spiritual energy. A group calling themselves psychic vampires do that—they are not vampires. I have never met a real one, but if they do exist, then they are a different species and should not be considered a true vampire. Just like a koala bear is not a true bear, but a marsupial. Don't let the name fool you.

Vampires do not eat a person's soul by having sexual relations with them. That is a succubus (female) or incubus (male). They are the ones who seduce the opposite sex to have intercourse with them so that they may feed off their souls, causing their prey's health to deteriorate and possibly kill them.

For those of you who believe everything you are told, vampires cannot eat chocolate cereal—even if it is vampire-themed. (A word of advice for any humans who might get ahold of this totally fictitious book:

Any cereal that has massive amounts of sugar is not part of a balanced diet for anyone—living or undead.)

Oh, and while we're talking about feeding myths, your eye color is not dictated by your diet. They are not gold if you feed on animals, red when feeding on humans, and turn darker as you get hungrier. Your eye color will stay the same unless you decide to wear colored contacts. And speaking of eyes, they do not cry blood. Although a cool visual for literature and film, in reality, it would be very wasteful of our body to dispose of our nutrition source so readily.

I could break down food and feeding myths forever, but you have more important things to learn. So let's move on to the hunting and gathering of blood.

III

Hunting: The Stalk-or-Seduce Response

Now that you know what you can and cannot eat, the next obstacle on your way to not dying will be how to get your feed on. There are several different techniques you can use based on unique factors and scenarios. Keep in mind one of the oldest maxims, "Man is the most dangerous game." Forget this, and you might find yourself in a very precarious position.

Literature, film, and lore often reference killing your prey to survive. However, you need not murder your victim. "Finishing" your meal does make covering your vampire identity easier, but it is not mandatory. Vampires need to consume a little over five liters of blood per week to maintain their health and grow stronger. This number can vary based on sleep habits, age, and health. I am assuming that you, dear reader, are a recently turned vampire, and so five liters will be your requirement for the first one hundred years. As you grow older, you will notice your ability to survive on less, but the cravings never go away. Major injuries will require immediate feeding. The amount of blood needed will depend on how severely you are wounded.

The average adult contains just over five liters of blood, which means that theoretically you only need to feed off one adult human a week. This also means that you will only have to dispose of one body a week. Think of all the extra free time you'll have! If you want to spread your meals over a larger population and not actually kill anyone, then you are going to have to cover your tracks and make sure that none of your human snacks become suspicious. The average amount of blood an adult human can lose before dying is two liters. Realistically, any more than one liter and your prey is going to notice that something is not right. Meaning, at this rate, you will have to cover five meals a week. Obviously, it is much more difficult to cover your tracks when you leave your meal alive as a witness rather than dead. To steal a line from my favorite amusement park ride, "Dead men tell no tales."

Either way, you will need to worry about the trail of death and destruction you leave in your path. On the upside, one thing you won't have to worry about is weight gain! We can eat (or, ahem, drink) as much as we want and never get fat! The downside is that we vampires do not lose weight either, so if you were turned before you went on that diet, sorry, it's too late. Fortunately during your initial transformation you will automatically lose a few pounds of flab right away. Your body becomes more physically fit due to the transformation.

PEARLY WHITES

With all your strengths and abilities, the single most valuable feature we possess in our hunting arsenal is our fangs. Yes, later we will discuss other things that help us in capturing our prey, but the fangs are what make us most effective at getting that succulent blood we need to survive. The obvious advantage to our fangs is their ability to puncture the toughest skin, which will come in handy if you ever crave a rhinoceros. The sharp points can sink directly into a major artery without killing our victims. Drinking from a living creature with the heart still pumping is ideal because the blood is guided directly along the fangs and into our mouths for consumption. The weaker the pulse, the more effort you will need to exert on actually sucking the blood from the body. By only using these two small entry points, as opposed to ripping out a chunk of flesh, very little blood is lost in the transfer. Not only is ripping victims apart a highly inefficient way of getting blood, but it also causes a huge mess to clean up. A less obvious fang feature is that they secrete a chemical that induces euphoria in our prey while we are feeding. Keep in mind that the time the venom takes to kick in can vary from almost instantaneous to about ten seconds, depending on the victim's age, size, health, and adrenaline level. Because adrenaline is the biggest factor in resistance to this venom, it is ideal to catch your victim completely unaware and relaxed. This will alleviate two of the major causes of adrenaline level spikes in your prey when you hunt: fear for their lives and the exercise they get when trying to escape. You will know when the venom has taken effect when your prey gives off a pleasurable moan. It is not sexual, but I am sure this is where a lot of the sexuality associated with the vampire legend originates. These pleasurable feelings will cease soon after your fangs are removed from the body. This venom also has medicinal properties that allow for the puncture wounds to heal quickly. They will not completely disappear, but there will only be a small red mark where the puncture was made. Bleeding will stop within moments and the wound will only take about twenty-four hours to heal completely. This goes a long way in covering up evidence that your prey was fed on by a vampire. One fact to keep in mind: This healing process will not work if you kill your victim. Once the body is dead, it can no longer heal, and thus evidence of bite marks will be left on the body. This may seem obvious, but keep in mind that some hair dryers have the warning: "Do not use in shower" or "Never use while sleeping." I don't want to be sued because some vampire out there has no common sense.

Your fangs do have the ability to extend and retract. At full retraction they will slightly stick out from your top tooth line. At full extension they will

Extended.

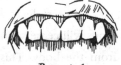

Retracted.

protrude about an inch. Even retracted they are obviously fangs, but will not draw attention to you unless you're flashing a big toothy grin. They definitely will not give you a speech impediment or scare the neighbors.

PUNCTURE POINTS

When drinking from your prey, it is recommended that you go for the major arteries. The one most commonly used is the carotid artery. It's located along the side of the neck and, if you have ever seen a vampire film, you can probably easily locate it. The nice thing about going for this one is if a passerby should see you, they would probably assume you are making out with your victim. Don't want to look like a teenage lover? The radial artery is located in the wrists. I prefer drinking from here because it offers the most versatility in terms of positioning, adding to maximum comfort as you drink. The least known and used feeding spot is the femoral artery. This is located at the inner thighs. Although it is an excellent location to receive maximum blood flow, its location makes it very awkward to get at, especially in public. This location is anything but discreet.

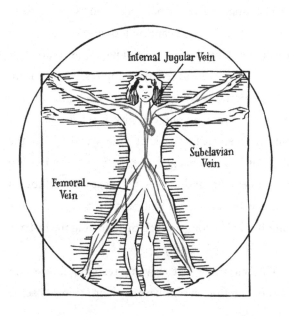

SEDUCE

Seduction will be your best hunting technique if you want to keep adrenaline levels in your prey low, though this technique requires the greatest mental skills. Yes, many vampires can use their powers of hypnosis to aid them, but only a fool would completely rely on these abilities. Besides, isn't it more fun to see what you can do with your wits alone? Every prey is a unique individual who needs to be read and responded to differently. Likewise, every vampire has different techniques and tricks that they rely on, but remember that you will have to be the ultimate player. It's important to note that seduction is not a technique that only the beautiful-looking vampires can implement. Granted, this technique tends to be most effective for beautiful female vampires. Men tend to be bigger suckers when it comes to falling for the opposite sex, but everyone can give it a try. The other thing to keep in the back of your mind is that the image of beauty changes over the years. Skinny may be in one year, and curves the next—so without a doubt, your body type will be all the rage at some point if you live long enough by following the instructions in this book closely.

The one thing that all vampires who choose this form of hunting should have in their arsenal is some kind of breath freshener. Being on a fresh blood diet creates the worst breath imaginable, which is where rumors of our foul odor arose. A vampire who does not take good care of their hygiene can smell like living death. Truly the worst cast of halitosis imaginable.

STALK

Many vampires, especially older ones, enjoy physically hunting humans down and then draining them dry. I have to admit, as civilized as I try to be, the taste of adrenaline-infused blood is delicious. Hunting is a great rush but probably the hardest thing to cover up and the quickest way to have rumors of vampires start spreading around your hunting ground. Always remember: Never hunt in busy areas—the less populated, the better. This is why small rural areas tend to have more of these monster stories than larger urban cities. If you find yourself living in the city, then you will want to find appropriate dark alleyways and places that vacate after dusk.

Large parks are a great place to hunt at night, since they are usually deserted except for vagabonds, criminals, and drug addicts. They also have a lot less artificial lighting to help your actions go unseen. Contrary to popular belief, shady parts of town are not the best places to hunt. There tend to be a lot more people on the street doing their illegal activities, which often garners a larger police presence. A plentiful hunting ground in the city is around the clubs and bars. Each city will have different times when they shut down, and generally last call will be well before sunrise. This is an ideal choice for hunting because there will be plenty of prey that will either be too inebriated to have others believe they were fed on by a vampire, or so desperate from their inability to attract a companion that they will be more susceptible to your charms.

FAMILIAR DIET

Using your familiar as a food source is probably the easiest way to find nourishment. If you're not sure what a familiar is, we will go into greater detail about these human lackeys in chapter 10. What you need to know now is that they offer a constant and willing source of fresh blood. However, this will depend on much more than your personality and vampire powers. This is where your mafia-like connections come in handy. The problem is not when you are feeding but for all the time they spend away from you. Yes, they may initially be faithful, but people are fickle. They may tire of being your meal on wheels. If they know they are being constantly watched, it gets rid of any ideas they may have about spilling your secrets.

So what kind of human can you trust? The best candidates for this job are those humans who want to be vampires themselves one day. Be forewarned: If you use them, it will be much like taking a long road trip with little kids. Rather than a constant drone of "Are we there yet?" it's going to be "Are you going to turn me?" Try not to break their neck. They have a hard job position to fill. Other great candidates are those with low self-esteem or extremely lonely individuals. They don't want to be a vampire, but crave the feeling of being accepted or needed. Their loyalty can be unwavering, but much like a scorned lover, their wrath can be even greater. I prefer to avoid these candidates since they tend to be emotionally unstable and way too needy.

Some vampires have a live-in familiar. This might sound like a great idea, but it is like having a high-maintenance pet. Sure, by living under your spell for so long they are your most loyal slaves and will do your every bidding, but they take a lot of upkeep. If you thought owning a dog was too much work, then I highly discourage you from going this route. You will have the usual responsibilities of feeding, grooming, entertaining, and providing for them, but you will also have to work hard on covering their trail. These pets tend to lose much of their former intelligence. They can still be somewhat smart but will do a lot of dim-witted stuff that can get you in trouble. Dracula's familiar, Renfield, is a perfect example. He was very bright before being put under Dracula's spell, but after, he starts to go around eating bugs and blabbing about his master all over the place.

BLOOD TAKEOUT

The most obvious and overused way to get blood is through transfusion bags from a local hospital or other medical facility. This is similar to buying shrink-wrapped meat served on a Styrofoam tray at your local grocery store. You know it comes from a human but you don't feel the guilt of how it was obtained. Each bag contains a pint or around a half liter of blood. You would need to supply yourself with ten bags of blood a week. If you do not have access to hospitals, many vampires have gone into business selling units of blood to other vampires. This can get expensive since you are dealing with a middleman. However, it is a very safe and reliable source once you find a trusted supplier.

Refusing to drink human blood makes finding food easier (though not nearly as fun). Also, you may find your hunter's instinct going unsatisfied, which may lead to some unforeseen consequences. No matter how advanced, all vampires have a primitive animal nature. Remember, to deny this is to deny yourself—this primal hunter's instinct may surface at a very awkward moment.

With all that pent-up energy, imagine what a vampire would be capable of when standing in long lines or stuck in traffic. A vampire with road rage will use a lot more than their horn or middle finger. Actually, they might get really creative with the talon-like nail located on their middle finger.

Pet stores are an excellent source of food. Consider them your fast-food restaurant. They have a plentiful supply of inexpensive, accessible food with few nutrients. You will have a large selection to choose from, whether it be mammals, reptiles, birds, amphibians, or fish. Larger mammals usually require a lot of paperwork and, if you are going in and buying a dog or cat every couple of days, people are going to start wondering what you are doing with them. Fish tend to die off quickly, so pet stores are accustomed to seeing people replenish their aquariums. **DO NOT** try to return fish you have drained of blood for free replacements. Saving money is not worth possibly exposing your true nature. Feeder animals like mice can also be bought in large quantities without drawing attention. If you must buy larger animals, I suggest spreading yourself around to different shops and animal shelters.

If the thought of using a pet store as your local

supermarket disturbs you, perhaps you should think of going free-range. Animals can be hunted the old-fashioned way with nothing but your wits and natural (or unnatural) abilities. This can be very challenging since animals, especially wild ones, are constantly on alert for predators. Their smaller size allows them to hide in places you cannot fit. Unlike hunters, you don't want to shoot an animal dead from far distances, since you will want to drink from their still-living bodies. It's quite an art to be a good hunter, and hunting is an excellent way to satisfy your animalistic side.

A less exciting way is simply to sneak onto a rancher's property and feed off their livestock. Although boring, there are still several things you need to be cautious of. If you have watched *Food, Inc.*, then you know that getting into these storage facilities is like breaking into a warehouse. It is not like the old days where you snuck onto Ma and Pa's farms and got a late-night meal. Animals raised for money are accounted for, and if they begin to go missing, die off, or suffer health issues, then there will be an investigation. This means that your feeding is the equivalent to breaking and entering into a place of business. Do not try to pull the "Is it wrong to steal a loaf of bread if your family is starving?" excuse. According to the law, you are a criminal and will be hunted down.

FEEDING TIME

Certain periods of the year when people fear evil monsters are the worst times to go hunting. People tend to be more cautious, and there are other creatures that hunt at these times. Full moons offer better light to your prey, and your chances of having to compete with a werewolf for food will significantly increase. On Walpurgis Night, April 30, people will be on high alert. It is a time when witches will also be gathered together for large celebrations, and it is always advisable to avoid magical creatures whenever possible. Magic has a tendency to negate many of your special abilities.

Halloween was originally a terrible time to hunt, but in many areas it has become so commercialized that it's turned into the ideal time to hunt, because people will think you are in costume. Those suckers will be so impressed with your realistic costume that they won't have time to know what hit them.

FEEDING MYTH BUSTERS

Before we move on, I must dispel one more rumor that has bugged me for years. We vampires are intellectual creatures. We are not mindless eating machines. You will not go berserk if somebody gets a paper cut on their finger or nicks their face while shaving. Yes, if you are starving this might pose a problem, but humans gorge themselves all the time when they are starving or on a diet. You don't see humans breaking down bakery shop windows to devour all the cakes they pass by. Like all other species, we deserve a little respect.

— IV —

Weaknesses:
The Older They Are,
the Brighter They Burn

Now that you've died once, it's pretty hard to be killed a second time. Vampires don't die of old age, but there are still plenty of ways to bite the big one. Thanks to mass media, many of our weaknesses have been made common knowledge. They have also done us a lot of good by spreading many myths about our weaknesses. I remember the first time I got holy water thrown in my face—it was like being on a bad date when the woman throws a drink at you. Though unlike on a bad date, I still got to enjoy my meal.

NATURE KILLS

Sunlight is the most obvious vampire killer. It burns vampires alive. I'll say that the biggest laugh I've had in a long time was watching vampires sparkle in a movie. Unless you like to dress in sequins, you will not glisten in the sun—char to death, yes, but not glitter. The good news is that it has to be the actual sun to kill you, not some UV flashlight. If somebody shines a UV light at you, it might give you a rash, but that's about it. Hollywood loves cool gadgets, but they only work in the movies. The other thing Hollywood likes to do is film in daylight, and they will imagine all sorts of creative ways to make this happen. Do not be fooled into believing you can go out in the sun by just wearing sunscreen or a magical amulet. Scientists have still not invented the SPF 5000 lotion that will completely block out the sun. Sunglasses and tinted windows will not work either. The only way to go out in the sun is to block all sunlight from reaching your skin, meaning extremely thick clothing all over your body. If you can see through it, chances are light can get through as well. Luckily for us, with the age of electricity and light-bulbs, we are no longer as confined and limited because of our aversion to the daylight hours. However, the post office and other government offices are still a royal pain.

Garlic is another big problem, and possibly what I miss most about being a human. Trust me, stay away from the stuff. It won't kill you unless you eat it, but expect a painful burn if it touches your skin—imagine delicious-smelling acid being thrown on you! If you see a room full of garlic or someone wearing a bulb necklace, it is best to just stay away. If you get close enough, the fumes will actually burn the inside of your nose—inhale too deeply and your lungs will even feel it. Luckily, if you drink the blood of somebody who has recently eaten a lot of garlic, it will not kill you. It will make you feel ill and want to vomit, but you won't die. Another lucky point is that you can notice garlic in the blood right away. It will taste spoiled and rancid. If you encounter tainted blood, stop feeding immediately and you may avoid any ill effects. Also, avoid passing through Gilroy, California.

Wolfsbane was thought to have the same effect on us as garlic. It does do wonders against werewolves, but we vampires are safe from that pesky little flower. In ancient times it was often used on the bite wounds of our victims and to wash poison from any

Wolfsbane

animal bites. As you now know, our venom is not dangerous, but helps heal the bite wound as well as releasing pleasurable feelings in our victims. This is much different from the dangerous venoms found in the animal kingdom, but humans can continue to use this if they wish.

WVD: WEAPONS OF VAMPIRIC DESTRUCTION

Beheading is the most common way for humans to kill us. It is not easy to cut off our heads, but it is the most accessible and logical way for people to attempt annihilating us. It requires little aim, and mobs always have plenty of sharp objects around. Exploiting most of our other weaknesses requires forethought and planning, but beheading can oftentimes be done on a whim. While mostly unsuccessful in face-to-face combat, humans can sneak up when we are unaware or immobilized. To avoid this death, make sure to keep your head attached to your shoulders at all times. As a note regarding our own self-defense: When in doubt how to kill an unknown beast, ripping its head off usually does the job. This is a huge weakness that we share with most creatures.

A stake directly through the heart is another fatal

weakness. The stake does not need to be made of silver, wood, or, more specifically, aspen. The aspen wood myth developed from the legend that the apostle Judas Iscariot was the first vampire and the wood used for Jesus' crucifixion was made of aspen. I wish it was that tricky, but unfortunately any stake will do. The stake does need to remain lodged inside our hearts until death, but humans staking us to the ground until we decompose is overkill. A little less than a minute is all it takes. Also, if the stake goes through your body and then exits or does not actually penetrate your heart, then you will survive. You will be paralyzed for a short time until the wound has time to heal, but you will not die. You will appear to be completely dead with no signs of life even though extreme pain will be shooting through every inch of your body. Many times people will just walk away assuming they are safe. You can eat them when you get back up. Not only does it give you a good feeling of revenge mentally, but their blood will make you feel better physically.

Unfortunately, those aware that we turn to dust upon death will use our moment of paralysis as an opportunity to finish the job. This is a perfect example of why the less people know about our true weaknesses, the better. If you see anyone approaching you with a sharp object, please be careful. A stake, though more difficult to deal a deathblow with, can be fashioned from countless common objects. I have known one vampire who discovered that the pen really was mightier than the sword.

We are extremely allergic to silver. No, this is not a result of Judas betraying Jesus for a bag of silver, but because of its elemental makeup. Silver compounds act as an antibacterial agent. (Little fact to make you look smart: Pioneers dropped silver coins into milk to keep it fresh.) For years we were able to cover up our aversion to silver by placing it heavily into werewolf mythology, but it will kill both of us. If you get silver

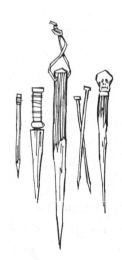

on your skin, as long as it does not pierce your heart or brain, you will be fine. The wound, however, will take longer to heal than one from any other compound. If the silver does not break skin, then you will get a painful rash that will last until your next feeding session. I mentioned that a lethal stake through the heart needs to be perfectly placed, but that is not

the case with a silver abrasion. Silver only needs to nick a major organ to knock us out. It works as a poison that spreads quickly, destroying the tissue faster than we are able to heal. My best advice is to not be distracted by shiny objects.

More bad news: Fire sucks for just about everyone. There is no way to heal from being burned to a pile of ash. Thankfully we are not as flammable as everybody believes. We may turn into dust immediately after being killed, but this is attributed to decomposition, not combustibility. It takes a lot more heat than throwing a match or torch on us. As of the latest version of this book, people are not carrying around flamethrowers or stockpiling napalm at home, and when that starts happening I think humans will have bigger concerns than vampires. It's safe to say fire can be deadly, but this should not be a large concern. If you are still paranoid about catching on fire, I would suggest only wearing fire-retardant materials. You may not be winning any fashion awards, but at least you will stop flinching every time someone lights a match. If you do catch on fire, my only words of advice are . . . stop, drop, and roll!

FOOLED YOU! MYTHS DEBUNKED

In brighter news, vampires can indeed cross running water. It was believed that running water was pure, and could not hold magic. Hence humans assumed that it would be impossible for us "magical immortals" to cross. Just because we don't hit the beach and enjoy a good swim doesn't mean that running water is deadly to us. An advantage to not needing air to survive is that we can stay underwater indefinitely. This is very handy when sneaking up on your intended victim or if you need to quickly get away from sunlight. If you never learned to swim, you do not have to worry about drowning, but watching a vampire doggy paddle is a little embarrassing. You lose a lot of your menacing presence to say the least. Better to weigh yourself down and walk on the bottom sediment underneath the water's surface. Mortals will be fascinated and frightened at the same time.

Humans also think that we depend on soil from the area of our vampire birth. Wrong! No, native soil is not where we draw our powers. If you plan on traveling a hundred miles from your native land, don't worry about packing that pound of dirt. It's a total waste of space. If you plan on sleeping in it, prepare yourself for an expensive laundry bill. Dirt is not easy to get out if you have been lying in it all day. It's a good thing this legend isn't true, because with the transportation available to us today this would be a serious crimp in our travel plans. Imagine trying to explain that carry-on item to airport security.

People's desperate attempts to feel safe have led to some great advantages for us vampires. They create myths out of thin air. We vampires can and do enter people's homes without being invited in. This myth sprang from the belief that a threshold was holy. Since we are considered demonic creatures, we would be unable to cross these barriers unless allowed in. Why this belief persists today, I will never know. Of course these are people who also believe a fat man can get down their chimney with a huge bag filled with presents. That being said, you should mind your manners and ask to be invited inside a home before consuming the family that dwells in the home. It is the polite thing to do. Remember, we are the undead, not animals.

UNHOLY DEMONIC CREATURE—NOT!

The evil, demonic creature myth has also led to other false beliefs of our weaknesses. Sorry, there is no grotesque monster hidden underneath our human form. Crucifixes, even those imbued with true faith, will not cause us to turn away in pain and horror. Unless it is being used as a stake or made of silver, you don't need to worry about it. The same goes for the Star of David or any other religious symbol. Holy water will not burn your skin, but it is very frustrating having to walk around in wet clothes for the rest of the evening, especially on a full stomach. We are not demons or some other religious entity—so religious relics offer no protection to our intended victims. What they do is persuade our prey to stop running and try to stand their ground. This makes hunting them much easier.

Holy ground is just like any other location on earth. There is nothing preventing us from going inside an area just because it is considered holy. Granted, many older sacred buildings were built more like fortresses than places of prayer, which does provide more protection. However, the belief that a place of worship will shelter people from "evil" often gives them a false sense of security. In times of panic they will flock to these locations, hoping to escape the horrors outside. In reality, all they accomplish is offering us a larger buffet to choose from. It is nice of them to make our job easier and gather so nicely like sardines.

OCD

Many cultures believe that by leaving large bags of grain, rice, pebbles, or large quantities of anything in our path will save them. Apparently we will be forced to count each and every one of these items before we can move on, thus giving them enough time to escape.

I have no idea who writes this stuff.

Unless like Dustin Hoffman's character in *Rain Man* you were obsessive compulsive about counting things when you were human, this will not be a problem for you. There will be no overwhelming desire to stop and count. If this were true, we would never be able to pass under a tree without counting all its leaves. There would be a lot more vampires burning up in the sun because they were too busy counting all the blades of grass. It is probably because of this myth that my favorite fictional vampire was created, Count von Count from *Sesame Street*. Finally, representation in the living world as someone who was not a blood-sucking demon! It would take many more years before humans would start accepting other good vampires in popular culture and allow them be portrayed by people instead of Muppets, but Count von Count is a true pioneer.

HUNGRY HUNGRY VAMPIRES

One question that gets asked a lot is: Can vampires starve to death? I do not have an answer to this question, but it needs to be looked at closer. While no vampire has ever died of starvation, many vampires have died because of their hunger. The older you are, the longer you can go without any side effects or weakening of your powers. The actual length of time you can go without feeding varies from vampire to vampire, but the order of the symptoms will be the same for everyone. At first there will be a slow decreasing of your powers. This puts you in a vulnerable position. Over time, using your strength and abilities becomes second nature, and many vampires have died during these times of hunger because they misjudged what they were still capable of doing. Leaping from rooftop to rooftop normally works in an escape, but you may not make the jump if your powers are depleted. In a weakened condition, many vampires have landed flat on their faces, smack in the middle of the pursuing mob. Your ability to heal will also be greatly reduced, turning what would have been an annoying scratch into a hindering obstacle in your escape. These first signs of starvation are serious and should not be underestimated.

The biggest danger to your survival lies in what

comes next—the loss of your mental abilities. We vampires are very intelligent and our long life-spans usually equate to vast knowledge. Of course, some vampires are illiterate and only learn to play the hunter role. However, these jocks of the vampire world are in the minority. The longer you go without blood, the less you will be able to focus on anything else, and the more you will turn into a dumb jock. If this goes on long enough, you will slip into a ravenous, berserker-like state. You will be driven by one desire: to feed. You will find yourself tracking down the nearest source of blood and tearing it apart with abandon. This behavior and mental state continues until your hunger has been completely satisfied. This careless time is when many vampires are hunted down and killed. In this state, vampires draw attention to themselves and often make very public killings, which can lead to angry mobs destroying them. If you are lucky enough to survive until your hunger has been satisfied, remain cautious. You may have drawn attention to yourself, and humans may be on your trail. Humans aren't always the smartest species, but knowing about your inner beast nature better prepares them to kill you.

When you leave this state of mind, you will have no recollection of what happened. Vampire instincts take over and you may come back into lucidity in the middle of a bloodbath. If you ever find yourself coming out of this mental state, don't take any chances. Leave right away! Find a new home and create a new identity. Vampires rarely fall into this berserker state, so do not let yourself fall victim. There is ample warning for you to find a source of blood before it's too late—even a rat will suffice.

The most common victims are recently turned vampires who refuse to drink blood. They think they are being moral, but end up causing more damage. Vampires who have become trapped in isolation, such as being buried alive with no sources of blood available, can also go berserk. Vampires in excess of a hundred years old have been known to place themselves into a deep hibernation and go indefinitely without needing blood. However, upon waking, they will need to feed within the hour or they quickly degrade into a ravenous state. This is why many stories of vampires being vicious monsters have come about: Humans have stumbled across a hibernating vampire only to awaken them and become their first meal.

VAMPIRE CURE

The saddest stories humans perpetuate are ones of vampires turning back to humans. Perhaps these rumors were started by mortals with loved ones who turned. If you kill the original vampire, all other vampires in the line will not return to human form. There are no physical or mental ties to the one who turned you, other than the standard relationship development. You also cannot burn the vampire out of you by using the sun as some sort of purifier. Once you are a vampire, you are a vampire till the end (even if it happened in Vegas).

MIRROR, MIRROR ON THE WALL

We have a reflection. Many vampires, due to eternal youth, tend to be very vain and stare at themselves obsessively. This myth probably sprang from us being effective hunters and able to sneak up on our prey unseen. People needing to rationalize things started to make excuses—for example, saying we did not have souls or that because mirrors were originally lined with silver, we would not cast a reflection. Only creatures as slow-witted as humans could come up with these ridiculous ideas. I was not sure where in this work to shatter the mirror myth, but since cultures tended to believe that it is a way to prove we are vampires before hunting us down, I decided to put it in weaknesses. Luckily this myth can be used to our advantage by putting people at ease and reassuring them that we are not vampires. This trick works every time!

MOSTLY DEAD OR ALL DEAD

Sometimes I can't relate to humans and their silly theories, but we do have at least one thing in common— just as their death is an unknown mystery, so is our passing from this physical world. I am not going to go into the philosophical debate regarding if we vampires have souls, or what happens to our souls when we turn from humans to vampires. That is a theological question. I am here to give you a lesson in survival, not a sense of meaning or purpose. I can and will go into detail on the physical process we go through when our bodies are destroyed.

We do not burst into flames, though it makes a cool visual effect in movies. In reality, we just quickly turn to dust. We do give off a quick burst of light when this happens, but that's nothing dangerous. It would not even give a human holding on to us a sunburn, let alone engulf them in a ball of flame. Could you imagine if we did burn up in flames? Just think about all the buildings and forests that would go up into smoke because we died in a particular location. We could have Smokey the Bear as a mascot. Remember, only you can prevent wildfires: Don't kill vampires in a dry forest. Joking aside, it is not a quick, painless death. Even if your head is cut off, you will go through extreme pain for several seconds before your body begins to turn to dust—one of the side effects of our super enhanced regenerative process. Hey, the best defense is a good offense. You're smart to read this book and avoid death at all costs. You'll be fine, as long as you take this book seriously.

Powers: With Great Powers Comes Great Fun

owers are tricky, even for us vampires. There are some that we all possess, others that we acquire with age, and several that come only to certain vampires. As a general rule, your strength and abilities will grow with time. It is a nice change from being human, where the older you are, the feebler you become, excluding studs like Sean Connery or Jack LaLanne. Seriously, I have no idea how those guys stay so young and virile during their natural lives, without being vampires! (Which begs the question . . .)

But I digress. You are reading this book because you want to learn about being a vampire, not so you can live a long, healthy, mortal life. As a vampire, your powers will begin quickly after turning. Once bitten, you are disoriented for a couple of hours, and then you will notice that you are in peak human condition. You can keep up with the fastest human runner, lift as much weight as the strongest earthbound bodybuilder, and have the reflexes and agility to match any mortal gymnast. You are in top form; however, unmatchable superhuman powers do not come for about a year, so hold off on challenging any Olympians to a high-stakes game. After the first year, all these abilities slowly increase. You will never be able to bench-press a tank, run on water, or balance on your pinky, but you will far surpass humans in every skill. In fact, you will eventually be able to achieve speeds faster than the human eye can process. This can lead to some very fun mind games. It can give the illusion of teleportation or being in several places at once. It also comes in handy when trying to catch your prey (or running away with your tail between your legs, for that matter).

THE FIVE SENSES

While you have to wait for speed and strength, your senses immediately become superior to any human's. They will not grow stronger as you age, but will become more instinctive and accurate as you learn to use them. Your hearing will match that of a cat and your smell that of a dog. That is to say, you can track prey with your nose as well as a dog, not that you will smell like a dog.

Although you will be able to see as well as a hawk, your true superiority will come from your nocturnal nature. Much like the owl or cat, vampires see extremely well at night. The side effect of this is that bright lights shined directly in our eyes give off a glow (much like the eyes of a cat or raccoon), because of the *tapetum lucidum* in our eyes. This is a dead giveaway that you are not human, so try not to get pulled over by the cops, who might point a flashlight in your

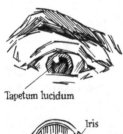

Tapetum lucidum

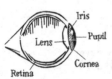

eyes, and do not stand in front of vehicles with their headlights shining. Actually, just avoid standing in front of vehicles altogether. It may not kill you, but it is going to hurt like hell.

This brings us to our sense of touch. Vampires not only have a better sense of touch than humans, but we also have a higher pain tolerance. We can take a lot of hits and keep going.

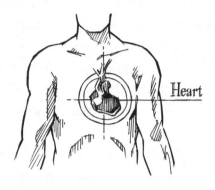

This comes in handy when rude people keep trying to stab you in the heart. It still hurts, but you will be able to fight them off for longer than humans can fathom. One great thing about modern society is that most people think our hearts are on the left side of the chest instead of in the center and only slightly to the left. We have the pledge of allegiance to thank for that. This misconception has saved a lot of vampires from human attacks.

Another way we are far superior to humans is our sense of taste. We can taste all sorts of subtleties, such as our victim's blood type or whether they have a specific illness. Another bonus to eating humans is that we can actually taste what they have recently eaten, and that can have some fun side effects. Because of our strong immune and rejuvenation abilities, we do not need to worry about bugs, viruses, or poisons in our prey, but we are not immune to all blood fillings. If you feed off a totally drunk frat boy, then you may feel tipsy for about an hour or so. Luckily, you get to avoid the hangover that would have followed if you were human. Please eat drunk humans responsibly.

Your body will also become more powerful with the help of new external features. We talked about fangs in the hunting section and will not be going into more detail except to say this: Never underestimate the importance of flossing. Remember, tooth decay is no longer a concern, but halitosis is. Your fingernails will also have the ability to extend and retract at will. They function like an animal's claws and are incredibly sharp and durable. They can cut through

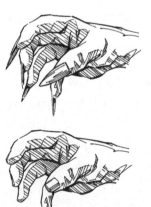

many objects like razor blades. However, they are not made of adamantine or some other fictional alloy, so don't try using them on a rock or metal door. Your toenails function in the same way, but they are a lot more awkward to use and, frankly, unattractive. I have never found a need to use my toenails in the few hundred years I have been around. Let me know if you find one though—I'm always looking for new material, and the sequel to this book won't write itself!

UNIQUE ABILITIES

It would be great if every vampire had the superpowers that you see in movies or read about in books. Sadly, not all of these abilities are true, and not every vampire develops every power. Some may grow over time, and some you may never acquire. Using these powers requires concentration and practice. It is not something I can teach you in a book, but I can let you know about some common powers so you'll know what you might expect. Most powers are discovered by accident, and being in mortal peril tends to speed up your learning process. I do not recommend putting yourself into that position on purpose, because if you do not have a required power, or are a slow learner, things can get ugly. This is not a movie montage where, after one emboldening song, you will be an expert—so have patience, practice, and pay attention to your intuitions. These new feelings may become new powers!

One exciting power you may acquire is the ability to control animals. It is said that we only control creatures of the night, but I believe this is because we are only active at night. Seeing how I do not wish to brave the sun and test this concept, it remains only a theory. The type and number of animals controlled depends on how intense your ability becomes and the mental strength of the animal. I use the term "animal" very loosely, and include insects and monsters of lower intelligence in the term. In the interest of preserving our street cred, you should adopt the phrasing too—saying you control animals sounds cooler than saying, "Hey, I can tell a moth what to do." Yeah, go have that moth eat somebody's Italian suit, that'll show 'em!

If you possess this power, the creatures will obey your every command. If you are strong enough, then they carry out these commands to their death. This requires enormous concentration, since self-preservation is a basic instinct that is extremely difficult to override (unless you control lemmings). This is a fun power to test in controlled situations—start by seeing if you can cause moths to battle to the death, or a group of zombies to break dance in unison, before trusting a larger beast to guard you.

Climbing is the most underrated power. Yes, you heard me correctly. Climbing is a special ability. I am not talking about climbing a tree like you did when you were a child, or scaling a mountain like an adrenaline junkie. I mean *really* climbing. You can climb sheer smooth surfaces as quickly as you can walk. It may not be as cool as flying, but most vampires have this ability. Usually it is the simplest tricks that are the most effective. It is highly recommended that you practice this ability going up from a low position to a higher one. Falling from a tall distance never feels good, and if you are going down headfirst before mastering this skill, you deserve what's coming to you.

All vampires possess some hypnosis power. It might just be emitting a soothing vibe to those around you, or you may be capable of having complete mental control of other intelligent beings. As you age, you will become stronger and more adept at using this power, but vampires will achieve their maximum potential at different stages of development. With that being said, there are things you should know about this power. Regardless of how hypnotically powerful you become, you must make eye contact with your intended victim during initial contact. When you have completely dominated the mind and will of a human, then eye contact can be broken and you may continue your manipulation, but they will be more susceptible to having your link broken. Also, some humans will have more resistance than others. For this reason you should always be cautious when attempting to control a human. Never assume they are under your complete control, or you might find yourself being manipulated by them instead.

If you begin to hear disembodied voices, don't panic. You're probably just developing the ability to read minds, or what is commonly known as "telepathy." This is a rare power, which is why I separated it from hypnosis. The ability to read another's mind is both an incredible and terrible power. It is wonderful to know exactly what somebody is thinking and what their intentions are. (By the way, if you have this ability, I suggest Vegas or Monte Carlo as a vacation destination.) But the problem comes with control and managing all the voices in your head. It is easy to be overwhelmed. Vampires who do not quickly learn to focus this ability often go insane. As with hypnosis, some beings will be more resistant than others. Vampires will always be harder to read, and to prevent them from knowing that you are attempting to read their mind is nearly impossible. It is highly recommended that you avoid reading another vampire's thoughts, unless you don't mind having your fangs knocked out. As far as humans go, just take it easy as you gently probe their minds.

No matter how powerful your telepathy or hypnotic powers become, you cannot wipe anyone's mind clear of events. Attempting to do so could result in the victim having intense physical or mental trauma. Also, vampires do not gain the memories of their victims as they feed, so that's another dead end if you're looking for an easy way to read minds. However, if you have the power of telepathy, your victims will be much more susceptible to your powers as you feed, thus they may give up more details than normal. Again, this is not because you are drinking their blood.

If you are a fan of party tricks, you will be pleased to hear that levitation is an ability all vampires possess to a certain degree. Only time will tell how powerful this will develop within you, but luckily, us vampires have time on our side. In its weakest form, this power aids in our ability to sneak up on our victims quietly and unexpectedly. We walk so lightly on the ground that we do not make a sound. You may be able to float vertically off the ground with limited side movement. The height and amount of side movement you can attain will depend on your strength in this ability. You will find this most helpful in reaching windows and doors that are above ground level, but this does not give you an excuse to be a peeping tom. It is useful for getting on top of roofs or other high areas while avoiding detection. Only a few vampires have a strong enough power of levitation to actually fly, but there is a neat workaround. If you cannot fly, a cool trick that takes a little practice is jumping from an elevated position and then using your powers of levitation to "glide" gently down to the ground. It is a total rush and will give the illusion of flight to those around you. A word of warning: Make sure you are able to levitate up to the height from which you jump, or it is going to be a rough landing.

Transformation may be one of the rarest of all powers. I have met very few vampires in my hundreds of years on this earth who can actually transform, but it can happen. Transformation usually comes in the form of animals—ravens, bats, and dogs are the most common, but there are countless possibilities. There are some incredibly exceptional vampires who can change into more than one form.

One form vampires cannot change themselves into is mist. This may be hard to believe, but the undead are not always the trustworthiest of creatures. Many use their speed to give the illusion that they are actually appearing from the fog, but it is all smoke and mirrors—pun intended. The lucky few who have control over the weather help support this myth by creating a fog before they appear. Which brings us to our next power.

Weather control is also a rare ability, and it's one that sounds a lot cooler than it turns out to be. Vampires with this power really just move some moisture and air around. This ability is more for mind games than anything else. You can water your roses, but you are not going to be able to flood a city block or anything that complicated. Moving fog in so that people can't see is a great hunting technique or escape method. Be aware that you are not going to be able to cover more than fifty yards, so don't count on it as your only exit strategy.

FALSE POWERS

Although you will be able to see well at night because of the *tapetum lucidum* discussed earlier, you will still need some light source. We give the appearance of being able to see in pitch black because our other senses are so heightened, but we do not have heat vision. It might sound cool, but this sort of sight would be a useless superpower. You would not be able to see the true color of the things around you, leaving you unable to enjoy the beauty of the entire world. It would also make bright lights extremely painful, and hinder you in your interaction with your prey. I know we vampires don't gallivant during daylight hours, but humans tend to congregate in well-lit environments. Think about how hard it would be to seduce someone while sporting red, watery, stinging eyes.

We vampires have received a bad reputation throughout history. Although it is an honor that humans believe we have godlike powers, they often oversell our strengths. Leave it to humans to look for someone or something to blame other than themselves. Let's start with my favorite.

There was a belief going around that vampires cause impotency. This is just men trying to make excuses for their own inadequacies. Suck it up and buy some Viagra, pal. I believe this is where the belief has spun off that we vampires are impotent ourselves. Since we do not reproduce in the usual way, our sexual desire is not as strong as it was when we were living. However, we are capable of having intercourse—it's just not for reproductive purposes. That's right, ladies: You need not worry about a vampire baby eating itself out of your womb.

Legends of the *dhampir* originally sprung from Balkan folklore, but these half vampires, with all of our powers and none of our weaknesses, do not exist.

We cannot cause blights or crop failures, nor would we want to. Even if we did have this power, it is not a good idea to starve or wipe out your food source. The idea that we would destroy mortals' means of survival, and thus ours, is one I have never fathomed. The reality is that vampires are concerned with a healthy human population as much as humans themselves.

I take it as a personal insult that we have been blamed for plagues and epidemics. Now, it is true that there have been a few vampires who have gotten a little gluttonous and eaten more people than they should have in a small area, but this is a rarity. I can't speak for all vampires, but generally we are a tidy and elegant species. Part of the reason for our survival has been our ability to get close to humans without sticking out. Hard to do that if you are a smelly, filthy pig. To counter the argument that we cause plagues, there are those vampires who take a moral stance against drinking human blood and would rather eat rats. This actually helps prevent the spread of disease. Maybe if there were more human-conscious vampires around in 1348, there would not have been the Black Plague.

One of the longest-running myths is the connection of our powers to the moon. It is in no way connected to our strengths. Moon rays do not bring us to life or heal our wounds. The moon affects werewolves, not us. Any time you hear a rumor about vampires and the moon, you can probably ignore it. People are constantly getting their mythologies mixed up, which is why this book is the only survival guide to trust. Remember to take note of your powers, practice honing them, and ignore any other stories humans tell. If you rely on the powers they think we have, you won't last long.

— VI —

Home Is Where the Coffin Is

This chapter title may be a little misleading, because you need not sleep in a coffin, and definitely not one filled with seven inches of blood. But now that I have your attention, let's talk abodes. Although not necessary, the coffin has always been an ideal place to sleep, especially before there were all the conveniences of modern construction and security. Sure, castles are great, but very few vampires could afford such a luxury. This is why the most common place to find vampires was in a cemetery—stone mausoleums were highly prized palaces for the middle-class immortal. Finding one of those was like winning the lottery! Contrary to popular belief, we never went back to our graves. Humans digging up coffins and destroying "vampire" corpses was a hilarious and futile effort in destroying us. Did people think we would spend the time to dig up and bury ourselves two times every night? That is a complete waste of time—even if we do have an eternity! There are many things we would rather be doing. And how could we rebury ourselves without disturbing the soil on top? C'mon, folks. We are talented, but not *that* talented.

But I digress—back to the hearth. Coffins are ideal but not mandatory. The advantage of a coffin is that it offers 360 degrees of protection from the sun. Even if a wall falls down or someone decides to open a curtain and brighten up the room, you will be well protected. Plus, a coffin is somewhat portable, so you can use it in your travels. Consider it a trundle bed for the undead. If you are nervous about security, add locks to the interior of the coffin so you can seal yourself in. Stick with locks that fit flush against the inside lining of your coffin. Padlocks tend to hang low and might whack you on the head. It may seem to be a strange bed starting out, but I highly suggest you give it a try. Coffins used to be very hard and uncomfortable, made of little more than wood. Today's caskets are a luxury item and can be more comfortable than most beds (especially compared with those found in college dorms or motels).

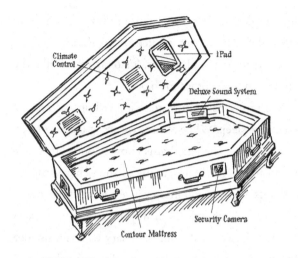

Climate Control

iPad

Deluxe Sound System

Security Camera

Contour Mattress

CLASSIC HOME OPTIONS

Castles were the dream location to live, because they offered so many of the amenities that we vampires would require. Solid walls are a must—you do not want any unwanted sunlight accidentally getting in and killing you. Castles are constructed with a good solid stone, while most houses of the olden days were filled with holes and cracks that would allow in light. The vast number of rooms in castles meant they had lots of storage space for accumulating riches. The labyrinthine layout of the rooms would offer added protection if anyone attempted to sneak in and kill you while you sleep. Solid doors and walls also meant it would take time to break into each room. The more time it takes to find you, the more time you have to either defend yourself or flee. Even though we are much stronger than humans, it's okay to run like the wind when one comes for blood.

We rarely have more than a few humans around where we sleep. While at rest, we are at our most vulnerable state. The less that is known about our sleeping locations, the better. Many of the richer vampires with lots of room and money invest in multiple identical coffins. This way, even if your sleeping quarters should be discovered, your adversary will have no idea which one you are in and be forced to open them one by one. If you do have the money and resources for this tactic, I also suggest nailing shut all the coffins in which you don't sleep. That'll really make them break a sweat. In a race against sunset, every moment counts, and for some reason people always try to kill vampires shortly before sunset. Why they don't just wait until morning when they have all day to look for us, I'll never understand.

Since most vampires could not afford castles, they settled for mausoleums, and this is still a great option today. In a way they are like miniature castles. The solid stone/cement construction meant a building fortified against outside intruders and elements. Most were built so that sunlight would not enter and there is usually plenty of extra room. This extra space can be used to store the things you will need for your nightly adventures, whether it be money or a nice change of clothes. We may not sweat, but that doesn't mean your clothes won't get stinky if you don't wash them. (Plus, eating people often shows on a shirt.)

Being located in a cemetery also helps, since very few people hang out at cemeteries after sunset, allowing an opportunity to slip in and out undetected. You might feel a little uncomfortable at first, crashing in somebody else's tomb, but they don't need it and it would be a shame to let such nice architecture go unappreciated.

VAMPIRE AMENITIES

In today's world, your options for what and where you would like your dwelling to be are almost limitless. Here are some important factors to take into consideration when finding your new home.

You will want to make sure there are several rooms that have no windows or doors to the outside. There should be no way for sunlight to enter. If you live in a house with no windows at all, people will start to ask questions, so don't get overzealous and board everything up. It only takes one nosy neighbor to get a mob started. I prefer homes with basements or storm cellars because they create a near impenetrable safety zone. Panic rooms are a nice option, but they can be very expensive. You will want to have your entire home battened down like a fortress. Security alarms are only the beginning. Think about reinforced doors, shatterproof glass, bars over the windows, and secret rooms or passageways as easy ways to slow down human intruders, but not hinder your escape if escape is necessary. The bigger, the better. You will most likely accumulate a lot of stuff over the centuries that would make any hoarder jealous. Also, for security reasons, more rooms add more confusion to uninvited guests. Another precaution that helps slow your would-be attackers is locking every door in the house. Some of these precautions may make vampires seem a little obsessive-compulsive, but many of the steps we take are for survival purposes.

Bomb shelters go in and out of style, but never rule out adding one of these to your property. They are buried deep underground and built to withstand bombs dropping. An angry mob won't stand a chance of getting in. If done right, it should not draw any attention to itself, though if discovered, people are more likely to think you are eccentric than a vampire. A cemetery with its own mausoleum might make people start scratching their heads.

LOCATION, LOCATION, LOCATION!

As with any real estate, it is all about location, location, location. You will want to be near an abundant food supply but not be forced to feed in your neighborhood. This will draw unwanted attention and make it necessary to move around more frequently. If you are reading this chapter, then you are probably looking for a semipermanent home and long-term survival.

No home will be permanent. You will be forced to move when your lack of aging begins to draw attention. Pro tip: Some places like Los Angeles—thanks to the plastic surgery craze—can be a home longer than others.

Wherever the place, it is a good idea not to return until the last person in the area who knew you or knew of you has either passed away or gone senile. This has a range of about forty years to almost a hundred. If you do not have a network set up in the surrounding area, err on the side of caution and wait ten years past the current life expectancy in the area. If you're in Japan, this might be a very long time, but if you are in Swaziland (the place on earth with the lowest life expectancy), it will be a very short wait. I would be remiss if I missed the opportunity to say there are many charitable companies and doctors who are working to help this poor country out. As a vampire, the health of the world is very important to us. We are as much a part of this planet as the rest of humanity. Take what you need, but help those out who are not as fortunate as you. Your future depends on the future of humanity. Let's not be like humans and squander our resources, taking them for granted until it is too late.

But forget about humans for a moment—let us get back to your survival. You will want to spread your homes apart, so as to cut down the likelihood of people from one area running into you at your new location. With travel becoming easier and cheaper, this can get harder and harder to accomplish, but you will want to cut down the odds as much as possible. Having homes in different countries is the ideal solution. You will want to avoid major tourist areas, places with small populations, or cities located within a tiny area. Chicago is big enough to compensate for the tourist influx, but Catalina could cause some problems.

LIVELY DECORATING

Avoid decorating your home with pictures of you from the past. Many awkward questions have followed when people notice an identical-twin-like resemblance to a person posing with Abraham Lincoln

or standing in front of the Eiffel Tower's construction. It only takes one person to question the distant relative story and start snooping around into your family history. It won't take them long to see that things don't add up. No offense to Marty McFly, but only in movies do people look and sound exactly like their distant relative.

It's important to give your home a bit of a human touch. You might invite people in as "dinner" guests and will want to keep up the appearance of a normal mortal. There are several simple things that vampires often forget to decorate or keep in their homes. Number one on the list would be bathroom supplies. Just because you don't have to use the restroom does not mean you should not have toiletries on hand. Another thing to remember is that due to our superior night vision, many vampires fail to properly light their rooms for a mortal's vision requirement, but a quick excuse can be that you are environmentally conscious and trying to limit your electrical use. Your dietary needs are very limited but you should still keep a fully stocked kitchen. This should not only be food, but cooking supplies too. Although you might never actually prepare a meal, kitchens usually have windows and are viewable from the outside. Keep your food items to nonperishables and remember things that people always run to their neighbor seeking, like sugar. Always be a good neighbor. You don't want to be that creepy person who lives in the haunted house or the first suspect when something bad happens in the neighborhood. Unless you live in Abbottabad, Pakistan, where it seems nothing you do to your house will attract attention.

Don't forget about your means of transportation. Sure, we vampires can move quickly, and some can even fly or turn into animals for faster travel, but people are going to start wondering how you get around town if you just start appearing. In most places, you are expected to own a car. You will want to get one that meets your needs, something nondescript that won't draw a lot of attention and is easy to maintain. There are not a lot of twenty-four-hour car mechanics out there.

Try not to let the stress of constantly moving

around get you down. It's true what they say, home is where the heart is—and it doesn't matter if that heart beats or not. Wherever you settle down, remember to stay secure, blend in, and don't eat the Joneses. Well, at least hold off until departing to your next place of residence—you might need their help moving!

VII

Finances: Nest Egg for Eternity

With an unnatural life expectancy, finances can be an even bigger burden than when you were expecting to retire at sixty-five. Trust me, there is nothing more pathetic than a vampire Walmart greeter. The tricky thing is that you must fly under the radar while still acquiring or saving enough money to live off of. It can become very difficult to explain to the IRS why at the youthful age of two hundred, you are not only still alive but able to work. You could say the only sure thing in a vampire's life is taxes. Somebody always wants a cut.

Creating a nest egg for a life of eternity can be difficult in today's world. It's harder and harder to commit financially beneficial crimes with all this new technology. With most money leaving an electronic trail, it is hard to save a large sum without people knowing where it came from and, more important, how long you have had it. We vampires as a whole really miss the era when all you had to do was pillage a town or hoard a treasure room full of jewels, rare metals, and priceless antiques. Although many of us still have spectacular collections of ancient artifacts and art, we can no longer use them as a steady source of income, because people start asking too many questions about how they came into our possession. Telling them that Leonardo da Vinci was a friend of yours just doesn't work as an acceptable explanation, even if it is the truth. Because of these obstacles you may be forced to work a job, even in your undead life.

I can't and won't be giving you any advice on how to commit tax fraud. The rules and investigation methods are constantly changing, so any advice I could give would probably be irrelevant by the time you are reading this book, and I don't want another audit. Auditors taste worse than lawyers and they rarely travel alone. It takes weeks to get the filthy taste out of your mouth.

There are several steps you need to take if you want to avoid detection. Yes, they are illegal, but as a creature of the underworld you can't be a saint and expect to survive. First and foremost, you need to make sure your savings are off the books. Your savings account is where the money trail ends. They find where you put your money away, and chances are they find you. This is why we vampires usually have a hidden treasure room sitting around where we live. With today's paper money it is much easier to travel from place to place. You thought moving was tough back when you were among the living? Try moving a couple of tons of gold, jewels, and other rare investments without being able to call a few buddies and bribe them with beer and pizza to help. And don't even get me started on getting the moving trailer back during daylight business hours.

Just like everyone else who was not born into money, getting it is the hard part. There are many different ways to go about doing this, but I will give you some of the more popular options that we vampires have chosen over the years. Unless you are feeding on the homeless, theft is the quickest and easiest option. You already need to dispose of your victim's body, and chances are they have some sort of valuables on them, whether it be cash, jewels, watches, or rings. If the authorities do by chance find the body, they will assume it was a mugging.

For those of you who are struggling with the morality of feeding off humans, I have a possible solution here—a good way to sooth your conscience is to feed off drug dealers and criminals. It's likely you will get mildly high after drinking their blood, but on the positive side you are getting rid of the scum of society. You can even pretend you are a superhero like Blade, doing the greater good. Drug dealers tend to have a lot of cash on them. Last time I checked, drug dealers still only accepted cash. Credit cards and checks were not the most popular forms of payment. This works to our advantage, since we are looking for an untraceable source of income.

If heathens aren't your cup of tea, many vampires today are going corporate. I don't mean opening a business—I mean they are a one-vampire corporation. That way no money is ever traced to them as an individual, but instead to an inanimate and eternal business. By forming their own corporations, they

have plenty of places to stash their fortunes, and it allows them to keep a pretty constant lifestyle. This takes a lot of work and is best suited for the workaholic. Now that I think about it this way, I guess businesses are people, and there may be a lot of Republican vampires out there. Who knew?

WORKING STIFF

Some vampires carry with them their need to feel productive and actually have a "job" that contributes to society. However, our inability to work during the day severely restricts employment opportunities. I will discuss some of the more popular options for employment but this is by no means all of them. It is just a short list to get you started.

The most common job you find vampires in is private investigation. You can do your investigation at night, and working alone adds a nice mystique. Our heightened senses, special abilities, and hunter nature make us ideal for this job. The only limitation is that you will not be able to take cases that require you to show up in court during the day. Sure, this means most of your cases will probably be cheating spouses, but if you want to warm your dead heart, locating missing people can be an admirable specialty. One of the side perks of this job is that you can fine-tune your hunting skills and get paid to explore the more seedy parts of town (aka excellent hunting grounds).

Night security guard is a similar job to PI, without the corporate independence. Again you get to avoid the daylight, and there is a lot of downtime for you to do what you want. After all, nobody is watching you—that's *your* job. The downside is that this can get extremely boring, and if the next shift is late or does not show, you will have to leave your post before sunrise. If this happens, the relief shift will not be the only ones losing their job, and you're back to square one. This career is usually chosen out of laziness or lack of creative thinking. Not because of the job itself, but because we vampires have so many other skills we can use to our advantage.

More and more vampires are turning to Internet-based jobs such as web design, support, and selling merchandise. It requires no face-to-face contact, meaning you can work from the comfort of your home and on your own time. This work gives you the freedom to hunt and enjoy the undead life. The biggest disadvantage to this job is that it is hard to cover your trail. Working in this field legally leaves a huge electronic footprint, so be prepared to cover your tracks.

Working in the health-care industry is another great option. People need medical attention day and (most important) night, so there will always be jobs

Count Domenick Dicce
Strada General Traian Mosoiu 26
Bran 507025, Romania
(555) 826-7473
Email: countdomenick@vmail.com

Education: **University of Bologna**
Civil Law
Cumulative GPA: 4.0

Objective: I wish to utilize my diverse job experience and special skill set to find innovative ways for a company to grow, while bleeding the competition dry.

Experience: **Family Farm**
Farmer
Responsible for maintaining five acres of land. Raised barley, olives, and grapes from planting to harvest. Job often required wolf population reduction.

Military Service
Recon Specialist
Specialized in night reconnaissance. Superior stealth skills utilized for intelligence gathering and target elimination.

The Leather Sole
Cordwainer
Was tasked with making luxury footwear
for the social elite, especially when new
shoes were needed overnight.

The Swan
Bartender
My extensive knowledge of mixed drinks
and liquor from around the world, along
with ability to read people, allowed me to
quickly serve patrons what they truly
desired.

Red Cross
Blood Processor
In charge of scanning donated blood into
computer database before it was sent off for
testing. This high security job was necessary
to prevent blood from being lost or
misplaced.

Sanguine Foods
Inventory Manager
Responsible for making sure inventory was
fully stocked at lowest possible price.

available and shifts that need covering. Few people prefer the night shift (when humans think all the crazies come out), so you could be the well-liked (im)mortal who takes all the graveyard shifts. The biggest advantage to these jobs is that you often have access to huge amounts of blood that doesn't require you to hunt down people. This also leads to the biggest disadvantage of being surrounded by lots of blood: It takes a huge amount of restraint to make sure you do not get tempted to treat your job like a Vegas buffet.

Speaking of Vegas, casinos can be an excellent place to work. Much like the medical industry, they are open day and night. Some of the best advantages are that if you can get a job that involves tips, such as dealer or cocktail waitress, it will give you a huge source of untraceable income. Don't be afraid to use those telepathic powers of yours to influence inebriated targets into feeling very generous. The biggest downside here is that, with all the security, your every move is being watched. What I find most disturbing is the disgusting smell of smoke and body odor from people who have been up all night. Not a very pleasant experience with our heightened senses.

I know this will probably cause an uproar, but I would not be doing my duty in preparing you for your undead life if I did not mention one of the oldest professions, not only in vampire history, but human history as well. Prostitution has been a staple career of vampires for years. Yes, you can get paid for it, but for lack of a better expression, many vampires just work for food. As vampires we never age or lose our looks, we are immune to disease, and we can easily protect ourselves physically, and customers tend to pay in cash. From a hunting standpoint it is the best trap we could set. Our clients follow us to a predetermined spot of our choosing. They are most likely embarrassed or ashamed by what they are doing, so they will cover their own trail. They will want to be alone, which gets rid of potential witnesses. When you are done you have plenty of time to clean up after yourself. While we're on the topic, this is probably a good place to take care of a couple of myths floating around. You will not lose control of yourself and tear your partner apart if you have sex. It can get intense and rough, but you have complete control. You have as much chance of killing someone during sex as you do when giving a hug. One is just a lot more pleasurable.

If you are living in a large city, taxi driving is an excellent career choice. Besides the good tips, there are many other benefits. People are not shocked with cab drivers exhibiting some odd characteristics. This job above all others will help you know your way around the city like the back of your hand. People will be jumping around the city, showing you all the hot spots and some dark, quiet neighborhoods as well. Chances are you will be getting drunks who not only can't drive but also would not remember if you took a little midnight snack from their neck. Just remember to let those intoxicating effects wear off before you start driving. You might be immortal, but your car isn't.

Cleaning crews are always in demand. This can be a nice, quiet job, and will have limited human interaction. Your levitation abilities can come in handy when trying to hit those hard-to-reach spots way up high. The biggest downside to this job is that the low pay and long hours will mean not having a lot of spare time to feed. But you will have access to all the supplies needed to clean up your own bloody messes.

You can always use your strength to work in the stockroom or on the unloading crew at retail stores. Physical labor is easy when you have super strength and endurance on your side. The biggest concern here is you will most likely be working with other people, and have to hide how little effort you are actually expending. Now you know how superheroes feel.

VAMPIRE TRADES

Many vampires have gone into business for vampire clients in a variety of trades. This offers a good source of income, and since you are dealing with other vampires, everything will be on the down low. Customer service is paramount if you go this route. Like most businesses, word of mouth will be your greatest advertisement, especially since you can't put ads in the paper or on television announcing what services you offer. Referrals and repeat vampire customers can sustain a business for a very, very, very long time. These services offered vary as much as your creativity will allow, so think of what you excelled at when human and you will thrive as a vampire.

If you are good with your hands, then being a handyvamp can be an excellent source of income that also brings a lot of variety. Vampires will have lots of odd construction jobs that need to be done with the utmost discretion. These jobs can range from having to build secret sun-proof rooms, a fridge used for blood storage, or deadly antihunter security devices. Whatever they are, each will bring its own unique flair.

Blood supplying is the most common business, because it is always in demand. Blood supply is the coffee

shop of the vampire world—the Starbloods, if you will. For this, you need access to black market blood, or you can set up a dummy blood donation center. Don't feel guilty about a fake donation center—they save human lives. But rather than giving blood to people who have already lost it, you are giving blood so people don't lose it in the first place. Think of it as a preemptive infusion. If you are still not convinced, then you should know that donating blood on a regular basis is healthy for humans. Research suggests that regularly donating blood can reduce the risk of cancer, heart attacks, and major cardiovascular events like a stroke. It also lowers iron levels in the blood, which may actually be a good thing. Too much iron in the blood accelerates the oxidation of cholesterol, which damages arteries. After donating blood the body has to replenish its supply, which helps a human's body stay healthy and work more efficiently and productively. Top that with getting a basic physical every time they donate, and it is a wonder more people are not lining up to donate at the Red Cross or their local hospitals. In other words, you help a human by setting up a faux blood donation center today! *This message has been brought to you by blood banks everywhere.*

If you're looking for another in-demand job, consider starting or joining a cleanup crew. The biggest downside to this job is you are the police of the vampire world and constantly on call. Rather than being ready to rush to the scene of the crime to collect evidence, you are removing the evidence. Vampires can be messy eaters, and blood is one of the hardest things to clean up. Most of us are not prowling around with a bunch of cleaning supplies, so you will never run out of work.

Entertaining can be one of the most lucrative businesses, because vampires love a good party. It is an exciting life requiring vampire and people skills, not to mention a lot of connections. This job revolves around entertaining humans and vampires in the same space, making sure the humans have no idea what is going on while providing a snack for your vampire guests. Over the years things have evolved. Ballroom dances and masquerades have turned into raves and costume parties. A *Bordello of Blood* has become a strip club open *From Dusk till Dawn*. You can still set up a brothel in rural Nevada, but your locations for operation are severely limited. Vampires still enjoy old-fashioned parties, but human clients always want something hip. Masquerades can still be fun, but at a costume party the vampire attire never goes out of style. If you throw a rave, never let clients convince you to use sprinklers to spray blood all over the room. It may be a cool effect, but the chaos it creates will only be more of a hassle than the cleanup.

Vampire relocation services are a vital business, but the profession requires years of training. This is not a business to start on your own. It is usually done through an internship, and any reputable business will be referral only. When vampires move, their new identity needs to be airtight. Vampires require new identities every time they outgrow their current life or seriously mess up one of their hunts. It is a tricky job requiring great skills and resources. You are not hiding vampires from the mob. You are hiding them from governments with vast resources.

Some creatures have decided to band together with mortals rather than stick with only their own kind. This was especially true when traveling circuses were popular. There are still a few around today, though they do not draw the massive crowds they used to. Nobody revealed their true identity, but they would use their unique abilities and appearances to fill the classic roles. Vampires often end up being the ringmasters because of their diverse skills and close resemblance to humans, but almost any job from strongman to acrobat to palm reader could be filled. This has been the one place today and through-out history where differences have been put aside and vampires, werewolves, witches, and even elves have come together to live in harmony.

While these are not the only jobs for vampires, they are some of the more popular options and are meant to get you thinking about your career. After all—retirement does not apply to the eternal!

— VIII —

Resting: Dead Tired

We may be undead, but we need our beauty sleep like any other creature on this planet. In our case, beauty sleep is probably not the best descriptive term, since sleep actually externally ages us. Remember, time is relative, so you can choose to snooze for days, months, or even years at a time. Be aware that long periods of sleep are more like being in hibernation than suspended animation. In the beginning there will be no physical differences, but after a couple of years of remaining asleep you will begin a slow aging process due to your lack of feeding. Don't worry—you won't look decrepit for hundreds of years, but you may notice a wrinkle or two before then. Even with the aging exterior, looks can be deceiving. You will still be far superior to any human you come across.

Short periods of rest lasting hours or days will allow you to heal faster. Just like living creatures' bodies use rest as a way to rejuvenate and heal, so do ours. This process happens down at the cellular level, so don't push yourself to stay awake when you need a good rest. Even if you are living in Alaska from November till January, you will still want to get a little shut-eye. Just remember that you *can* have too much of a good thing.

If you decide to stay up while the sun is out, you will not notice any difference at first (as long as the sunlight does not touch you). Your powers will not diminish immediately. You will not feel sluggish or tired. Just as the moon does not give us powers, the sun does not take them away. However, the lack of sleep will catch up to you just as it did as a human. While asleep, not only will your body be repairing itself, but it will also shut down so as to conserve energy. This is why you are able to go for longer periods of time without having to feed and not suffer many ill effects. To the outside world, you will appear to be dead as a doornail, while in reality you are simply dead asleep.

SLEEP CYCLE

Our sleeping process itself is unique. We do not instantly fall asleep and become stiff as a board when the sun rises, but we are able to put ourselves to sleep within seconds at any time. No more insomnia as you toss and turn, hopelessly trying to fall asleep. The process requires focus. Just bring your body and mind into a deep state of relaxation. Once asleep, we will appear completely dead to the normal senses available to humans. We do not go through the REM stage of sleep nor have any dreams. Your body will sense the sunset and wake up when it is safe to venture out. This has been accurately portrayed in popular media with the exception of vampires slowly rising into the sitting position. You will get up however you like—I am more the "roll over and get out" type, but some like to show off by leaping straight up into the air and onto their feet. Your eyes will suddenly open and all your senses will become instantly aware—truly up and at 'em! No more stretching, hitting the snooze button, or having to drink that first cup of joe before you wake up. Of course, if a guy named Joe is near you, there is no reason not to enjoy your first meal of the night!

Going into an extended sleep is a bit more complicated than just resting for the day. You begin with the same focus as normal, but halfway in you want to concentrate on the number of nights you wish to sleep through. Once you have this number firmly in your head you will want to visualize yourself waking up in this time frame. Think of the temperature for that season along with the sights, sounds, and smells you associate with the time you wish to arise. Once all these things are firmly locked into your mind, you may complete your relaxation until you drift to sleep. It may sound easy, but to keep all those thoughts in your head while maintaining your relaxation level can be quite difficult. I recommend finding times to sleep through one or two nights and gradually extending it till you can go six months with ease. If you can go six months, then you will have mastered this for any length of time you desire.

GOOD DAY, SLEEP TIGHT, DON'T GET STAKED

There are many reasons you may want to sleep longer than a single day. The first is boredom, on which I will go into more detail in the chapter Eternity: That's a Long Time. I always recommend sleeping through long trips. Some vampires enjoy these long travels and want to experience the journeys, but feeding becomes an issue. It is not the price of eating out concerning us vampires, but the attention it draws. Trust me, it's not easy!

It is nearly impossible to hide all your meals on a boat. Even throwing them overboard is not recommended, since bodies float. If you are traveling by land, chances are you are going to be leaving a nice trail behind, since you will not know all the areas well enough to consistently cover your mess. If you are flying, chances are you will be shipping yourself as luggage. Sitting in a plane causes too many safety concerns and temptations. Also, new security measures will probably notice something "strange" about you, and being delayed leaves the possibility of landing when the sun is up. Last but not least, with your heightened senses, there is nothing worse than being crammed in like sardines with a bunch of sweaty, ill-tempered humans for several hours. While the cargo area is more ideal, it is still an undesirable way to travel. If you thought flying coach was rough, then just wait until you are in the luggage compartment of an airplane. Sleeping is the best option, but there are still too many unknowns. Unless you own your own private jet, I would avoid air travel altogether.

Not all of us have the means to travel for extended periods of time, but you still may need an extended nap. One big reason is overhunting. This is especially common in smaller towns with little population growth and gossiping neighbors. A long snooze can help the area repopulate and calm the rumor mill. Fear can clear a town as fast as any natural disaster. Another reason you may want to sleep is an eclipse, so keep a close eye on the astrological calendar. An eclipse alters the time you can safely walk around and (in my opinion) it's not even worth waking for. It is frustrating and dangerous to wake up and go out on the town only to realize that it is actually the middle of the day and you have no way of getting to a safe location in time before the sun comes out. Trust me, always keep up to date with the *The Old Farmers' Almanac*, it has information on sun up/sundown and has been an amazing tool for me in planning my evening and travel plans in advance.

Vulnerability is the biggest downside to extended sleep: Almost nothing wakes you before your scheduled wake-up time. You are dead to the outside world. It does not matter how much noise people are making as they tear down your doors with axes, or how bright the light they shine in your face is. Mobs can throw holy water on your head or probe your body and you'll keep snoozing. You will not wake up until they have actually stabbed something into your body. Unfortunately, by that time it will be too late to defend yourself. My best advice is to secure yourself in an alarmed house, locked basement, or hidden passage and pray that any mobs who may find you failed anatomy class.

— IX —

Social Structure: We Are Family—I Got All My Vamps with Me

We vampires are not typically social creatures, but like any group in the animal kingdom, we follow a natural structure and set of social norms. Many of these stem from our human origins. Remember, we were all human at one time or another.

First and foremost, we respect our elders, which has nothing to do with etiquette. This comes from a sense of self-preservation. As we grow older, we grow stronger, meaning the older the vampire, the better the chance he or she can kick your ass. Show some respect and you might just live to be an elder yourself one day.

THE COVEN

Covens are a group of vampires who have banded together for any number of reasons. These groups may also be referred to as a House or Household, or by the more popular term Clan. Their reasons for forming could be as simple as geography or being turned by the same vampire, much like a human family. It could also be for more complex reasons, such as a similar set of beliefs, ideas, and traditions. Whatever the reason, they all have their own set of rules that must be followed. And don't let the term "group" fool you. The group number can vary from three to several hundred. Basically any time more than two vampires join together, it becomes a coven—after all, three is a crowd!

There are no requirements or formal set of rules for forming a coven, but most will probably have a few traits in common. The first one is obvious: The oldest or strongest vampire will be in charge. Most covens do act like a democracy, where all members have an equal say in the decisions. However, that does not negate the fact that the older, stronger vampire who has the power to rip your head off as easily as tearing the wings off of a fly will hold a little more sway in any discussion.

A vampire usually joins a coven for two reasons. The first is for protection. We may be physically and mentally superior to humans, but they will always outnumber us. Plus, there are other things out there besides vampires that go bump in the night. The second is a feeling of isolation. This is more common with younger vampires, and these feelings tend to disappear as you get older. Belonging to a coven does not mean you have to live together or always hang around each other, but members do offer support. With that being said, leaving a coven permanently is often a difficult and dangerous process.

Each coven will have a set of rules that need to be followed. These rules can never conflict with the Supreme Laws that all vampires must follow on pain of death. (Don't worry about those yet—I promise we will talk about them at the end of the book.) Although coven rules can be as varied as human laws, most of them will deal with the way vampires within your coven are treated. How each coven wishes to enforce these laws is up to them.

A sigil is usually used to represent the coven. In case you were curious, a sigil is a symbol created for a particular magical purpose and consists of a combination of specific symbols and/or geometric shapes each having a meaning behind them. In reality, they

are not magical, but a way to quickly mark property, territory, safe houses, or gathering locations. It is easily identified by other vampires and will not require them to read the language primarily used by a particular coven. It is the ideal marker and warning sign.

If two covens are going to occupy the same geographical area, it is a good idea for them to get along and work together. If you thought the Hatfield and McCoy feud was bad, with a mere twelve people killed, you ain't seen nothing yet. Feuds between covens have been known to destroy small cities. Yes, I used the plural—"cities."

Joining a coven is not a requirement. The decision to join is completely up to you. Of course, some vampires you come across will encourage you to join their coven by making an offer you can't refuse. This is not a fraternity/sorority you only need to deal with during your brief time in college. A better comparison would be to that of a crime family. If you decide to join a coven, make sure to examine your reasons thoroughly. Do as much research as possible on the actual coven itself. Researching the coven can be difficult, since you can't just search Wikipedia for the information. These organizations are secretive and gathering information will require all your investigative journalistic skills.

— X —

Familiars: A Vampire's Best Friend

Let's get one thing straight: Familiars are not friends. It is more like a dog-to-master relationship than anything else. Instead of fetching your slippers, familiars fetch your blood supply. They are human servants who want to become vampires, and after a period of long faithful service, you turn them. Think of it as an apprenticeship for vampires. Of course vampires do not reveal a lot about being a creature of the night, so it is up to the familiar to be observant. Since secrecy is our greatest ally, stay vague and redirect if pressed for an answer—like a human politician. If familiars begin to ask blunt questions or won't accept your reserve, it may be time to put an end to your arrangement. As a vampire, you have the upper hand, and just because you made a promise to turn them does not mean you have to keep it. After all, it is their fault for trusting you in the first place. Unlike lawyers, you really are a bloodsucker.

FAMILIAR'S JOB DESCRIPTION

Why do you need a familiar? Power is not a problem, but there are a few minor obstacles when it comes to fitting in with society. The biggest one is that the sun will kill us, and that makes going out during the day difficult. If you thought trying to take care of business with a nine-to-five job was tough, try taking care of things after sunset. The main job of your familiar will be that of your personal assistant. They take care of the things you can't do during the day, like mailing a package at the post office or picking up dry cleaning. Thanks to the Internet, many tasks can now be done at night, but familiars are great for any tedious tasks that would waste your valuable time. Personally, I hate going through e-mails that are offering a high school diploma and pills for improving my male inadequacies (as if I have any of those). Spam mail topped with annoying telemarketers has inspired me to use my familiars as communication buffers at all hours, but you can use them to manage any undesirable societal obligations. Tell you what, have your familiar call my familiar, and we'll have a bite for dinner.

TO DO LIST

☐ Mail package. This time remember to use post office outside my zip code.

☐ Drop off dry cleaning. Make sure they get rid of bloodstain on left collar.

☐ Pick up five blood transfusion bags.

☐ Bury body being stored in car trunk.

☐ Fill car with gas. If you forget again, the car won't be the only thing running low.

The second big drawback of living in society is that we require blood to survive. This is a repulsive trait to the humans you live among. Familiars are a great resource for doing some remedial reconnaissance work. Nothing too advanced, or else you risk exposure for their incompetence. Remember, if you want something done right, you will want to do it yourself, but a familiar can be more than capable of finding ideal areas to feed, picking up valuable gossip, or performing other law-abiding tasks that won't attract unwanted police attention to them. Remember, vampires are not the only ones to break under a hot light. Even the most trusted of familiars has the capacity to crack.

FAMILIAR JOB POOL

Where do you find these trustworthy assistants of the underworld? You can't put an advertisement out in public, though it would be hilarious to read the personal ad. I can see it now: *V seeks single VPA to help with daytime tasks, must not be squeamish around blood.* No, that won't work. You have to be subtle! The most obvious place to find your worker is goth/vampire clubs. They are popular right now and there will always be these groups floating around somewhere. Obviously, real vampires like you and I would never go to these places for fun. They are an excellent place to find familiars or a good meal, but entertainment-wise they are rather insulting. First of all, not all vampires dress in all black. As a fashion statement you will want to avoid black and other dark colors because of our pasty complexion. That is unless you spray tan, in which case I suggest avoiding orange-colored outfits, but I digress. When you are in these clubs you want to scout out older members.

Those who are closer to their teens than their thirties tend to be going through a phase, and you do not want a familiar outgrowing vampire adoration on your watch. Avoid teenagers in general. Their parents don't want to be around them, so why would you?

The homeless are another excellent source for potential familiars. They are not as well connected as club-loving folks, but they have other advantages. Being in a desperate situation, they will be more grateful for the honor of being able to serve you. Since they are without a home, these familiars can be good live-in house servants, always at your beck and call. Due to their transient lifestyle they can follow you anywhere and not be missed. Most people dismiss the homeless as crazy or on drugs, so if something should go wrong and they start screaming "vampire," nobody will believe them. With that being said, vampires know to never underestimate or dismiss anyone—including the homeless. Always treat them with respect. They are human beings and can work as well as anybody else. They just need a little positive attention and the right opportunity to succeed.

FAMILIAR VETTING

Just like you would not marry someone after the first date, you are not going to make someone your familiar on your first meeting. Get a feeling for them first. Run a few tests to make sure they are up to the task. Make vague innuendoes about vampire life and gauge their responses. A lot of people out there will think they want to be a vampire or a vampire's assistant, but chicken out when the opportunity presents itself.

To lower your chances of presenting the opportunity to the wrong person, you must do reconnaissance from afar. Find out what kind of person they are when nobody is watching. After all, they will be your biggest asset or hindrance when you are unable to move around. This is a good time not only to figure out what makes them tick, but also to discover their weaknesses. Everybody has vices, but look closely at those of a potential familiar. You want to figure out if you can use them to your advantage, or if these bad habits will be a dangerous liability.

While nothing is foolproof, I can identify several desirable traits in a potential familiar. Introverts and loners are great prospects. Their private nature works well for a life of solitude, and they are less likely to spill secrets to the local townsfolk. When working with a social animal such as humans, it is important to realize that you will not only have to be aware of the person of interest but also all those they are around. Coworkers, friends, or family members will ask questions and notice behavioral changes in your familiar, so it's best if your servant has a slim community of confidants.

Physical health is a very important (albeit often overlooked) trait. I am not talking about physical attractiveness, but actual fitness. Many gorgeous models obtain "beauty" thanks to drugs, starvation, or other rituals that put them in extremely poor health. Since familiars will be a steady source of blood, you want them in good shape. Not only does healthy blood taste better, but the healthier they are, the more tolerant they will be of having large amounts of their blood drained on a regular basis. Despite what two thousand years of ancient medical practices believed, bloodletting is not a cure-all to most diseases. It is taxing on the body to be constantly low on blood, which is why people must wait eight weeks between blood donations. Yes, donating blood is healthy, but anything in excess is not good for you. Humans have been known to die from drinking too much water and are much more fragile creatures than we vampires. The best way to keep familiars physically resilient is to start with healthy ones.

PROMOTION OR TERMINATION

While no vampire-familiar relationship lasts forever, rarely does a vampire actually turn a familiar. Vampires and humans have a different view on the passage of time. More often than not, the familiar will grow impatient and begin to act out. This usually happens because they no longer want to be a vampire and do not agree with the lifestyle, or they feel ready to turn and are no longer satisfied with simply being your familiar. Always be on the lookout for the warning signs before it's too late. Some common signs are less enthusiasm in doing your bidding or asking a lot of questions about why the job is necessary. Questions are common at the beginning, but they should soon learn that this is not acceptable. They are to do as you say without question. If they are asking too much about vampire specifics, they must be reminded that full knowledge is not given to familiars. Much like a pet, they will need obedience lessons and must be watched closely. Rather than rubbing their nose in the puddle of piss on your Persian rug, harsher discipline will be required. Humans are creatures of habit. If you notice a drastic change in behavior, be on the alert. This probably means something big has or is about to change in their lives, and thus yours as well. Make sure the change is not them going from vampire familiar to vampire hunter.

XI

Friends:
Who Needs Enemies?

Keep your friends close and your enemies closer.

What did you expect? Drinking others' blood to survive does not get us invited to a lot of social engagements.

— XII —

Enemies: Judged by Quality

I t is true that vampires do not have many natural friends in this world. Maybe that's a symptom of drinking blood to survive. People fear what they do not understand, and we bloodsuckers value our privacy. We're also one of the most powerful creatures on this planet (humble too, of course). It is natural for dominating beings to be feared. Therefore, we must discuss certain enemies so that you can be on guard and ready to defend yourself should you ever encounter such a threat. The worst blunder you can make is underestimating or misunderstanding your enemies.

WEREWOLVES

Let's start with a beast dominating the box office of late: the werewolf. When meeting a new werewolf, stay guarded until you know him/her as an individual. Today, many vampires and werewolves become the best of friends and have even been known to become romantically involved. However, we have long-standing bad blood between us (pun intended). This hostility is our fault, though most vampires will never admit it.

Long ago we enslaved werewolves and used them as our guards. Some vampires called them servants, but the fact is many werewolves never had a choice as to whether they wanted to serve us. Although they are physically stronger than we are, we possess many other talents that make us far superior, and this went to our heads. We started seeing them as inferior creatures or mindless beasts. They are not the smartest tools in the shed (especially when in werewolf form), but to underestimate them was a horrible mistake. Keep anyone down long enough and they will eventually rise up. And rise up they did. The Vampire-Lycan War was brutal and almost destroyed us both. Since vampires have a long life-span, some are still alive from the time of this war, and many carry grudges. It's a shame when I see an elder vampire fostering the hate and prejudices from that era. Although no werewolves from that time are still alive, current ones remain leery of friendly vampire intentions. Needless to say, we all have some trust issues, which can lead to unnecessary fighting. Just make sure you develop a genuine relationship with a werewolf before trusting him/her and you'll be fine. Also, don't try to eat them—it's time to bury the hatchet.

HUMANS

Our most dangerous enemies are those pesky humans. We eat them, but—much like cobras and mongooses—sometimes food bites back. Okay, humans do not literally bite us back. They will not drink or sell our blood as if it were a drug on the black market. Our blood does not give them accelerated healing, an enhanced libido, or increased strength, speed, and senses. However, when threatened, humans can turn violent. A human's natural instinct is to kill us on sight, not to get to know your personality. Although we are superior to humans in almost every way, their ingenuity and resolve can be stirring. Their greatest advantage is the ability to function in both the day and nighttime hours. That, combined with their superior numbers, has caused the downfall of many vampires.

Many humans throughout the ages have tried their hands at being vampire hunters. Most have short careers, but a few have found success. Back in the late 1800s (thanks to the popular Bram Stoker books) hunters were well armed and plentiful. Vampire hunters would carry a shovel, an ax, wooden stakes, and a mallet, but then they wised up. Professor Ernst Blomberg created a vampire hunter kit around the same time *Dracula* was published. The kit was constructed of a walnut box with a cross carved on the hinged lid. This box contained a pistol, ten silver bullets, a wooden stake and mallet, a crucifix, a rosary, several vials of

garlic powder, and serums thought to stop demons. Although not all these items were harmful, several were dangerous enough to cause us concern. Many travelers in Europe would start bringing these along on their journeys, which created a huge dent in our meals-on-wheels program.

Vampire hunters have generally decreased in numbers because of modern science "proving" we do not exist, but every now and then we see a resurgence. There have been many monster hunters in popular media (like Van Helsing, Blade, Buffy, and the Winchester brothers) that have inspired a new batch of vampire hunters. Lucky for us, vampire hunting in real life does not resemble these action-oriented movie techniques. So many of these hunters come in expecting to tear through hordes of us like we are inconsequential henchmen in some Hollywood blockbuster. In reality, smart hunters are stealthy and track us during the day. They hunt with plenty of daylight to spare, not moments before sunset. The vampire hunter who kills you is going to be the one you never saw coming. The ones who try to fight us in direct confrontations typically do not survive. After all, humans are insects to us when it comes to a fight. Humans do cause a problem when they attack us as a mob. Many vampires have made the mistake of standing up to an attacking mob, thinking of them as gnats, but with such overwhelming numbers, chances are one of them is going to land a lethal blow.

VAMPIRES

The lethal enemy you might find most surprising? Ourselves. Yes, we have a law about not killing other vampires, but the fact remains that more vampires are killed by other vampires than all other species combined. This is where the vampire psyche comes into play. When somebody goes from being human to a powerful immortal vampire, many psychological effects can take place over time. Growing into powers can make vampires feel invincible. They feel like no force on earth can stop them from getting what they want. They then attempt to rule over all vampires. In the past, many wars were started because one vampire felt he or she should be the supreme ruler. This has never gone well for them. They soon learn that they are not indestructible, and they are no match for the mob of vampires they suppress. Another enemy is the vengeful vampire who hates their existence and wants to destroy what they have become. This usually happens before they come into their powers (meaning they are killed quickly) but they almost always take a few vampires to the grave with them. Then there are the depressed vampires overwhelmed with immortality who don't harm anybody but themselves. Still, this creates a huge problem if somebody sees them disintegrate in the sun. Death by sunrise (aka sunicide) is the most popular form of vampire suicide. It has to do with the longing to see one last sunrise before they perish. Personally, I would probably go with an extra garlic pizza pie.

ELVES

Elves used to be a bigger problem for us than they are today, but you still need to be cautious of them. These Goody Two-shoes think of themselves as divine beings who are a force of good and protectors of this world. The problem is, they view us as evil entities that need to be removed. Top that with their magical powers, superior reflexes, high intelligence, and longevity, and they may be one of our most dangerous threats. Luckily these days they tend to stick to their own territory. There was a time when they left their land and went out into the world seeking adventures, but they got a bad rap. If they aren't delivering presents on Christmas or baking cookies in a tree, no one likes self-righteous magical elves. They got the hint and decided to stay in their own villages. As long as you do not stumble across their domain, they should not be a problem. If you do happen to find yourself in their home, run like Forrest Gump and get the hell out of there.

THE REST

A vampire must always stay alert. The species listed above are the ones you should take the most precautions around, not because they are the only ones who want to see your head taken off, but because they have historically caused us the most problems. Zombies are nobody's friend, but they are not a threat to us vampires. We have actually been able to use them to our advantage over the years as mindless guards. Leprechauns are only obsessed with their gold, so stay away from that and you will be fine. Just in case, consider everyone an enemy until you know them. Constant vigilance is necessary if you wish to live a happy and long undead life.

— XIII —

Turning Someone: To Love or Loathe

Turning someone into a vampire should not be taken lightly. There are many factors to consider before attempting this step. Why are you turning the person in question? Is it out of true love or just a passing infatuation? Both parties involved need to seriously consider every aspect of what is about to be embarked upon. Mortals can be captivated with the whole eternal love thing and not actually comprehend being with the same individual FOREVER! Many marriages don't last, and that is only for the brief human life-span. Perhaps you want to turn terminally ill people and save their lives, but you can't ask humans on their deathbeds if they want to be turned. The dying person will not make a rational choice. In the medical and legal world this is known as being of sound mind, which they are not. Is the person you are about to turn capable of handling the powers and mental strain they are about to endure? Being an immortal takes a strong constitution, as you are about to discover. It's not easy going from being human to eating humans. There are tough psychological stressors ahead and a weaker person will snap under the pressure. To see a vampire go crazy makes the term "going postal" seem tame.

THINK BEFORE YOU TURN

Before turning someone, think about the experience you had of watching those you knew in your past life growing old and dying. Remember the new friends you have made as a vampire becoming old in front of you and then leaving this world forever. Being forced to move from place to place before people notice that you are not aging. This is a deeply, deeply, deeply depressing experience. Is it something you want to share with someone you supposedly love, or even just like? There needs to be serious conversations before even considering a turn. Sorry, gentlemen, even the undead need to have "the talk" at some point in their relationships.

Never ever turn anyone against his or her will. This always leads to problems. People turned into vampires without consent are not mentally prepared for it and frequently develop psychological issues. Most of the time they are not outwardly destructive, but they are still a pain to be around. They just walk around moping about how much they hate themselves, how they're cursed, how they're doomed, blah, blah, blah, whine, whine, whine, bitch, bitch, bitch. They are big crybabies and are annoying to hang around for centuries on end.

A worse outcome is when they turn with a chip on their shoulder. They become obsessed with revenge and go vigilante, hunting down any vampire they can find. They make it their life's mission to either wipe out every vampire on the face of the earth or not rest until they kill the one who turned them. This not only causes a huge problem for you, but also gives the rest of us vampires a headache in trying to deal with the mess you created. After we finally fix this problem, you will be taken care of next. Not turning someone against their will has never become a law, but I have been lobbying for it to become one for some time. It keeps getting turned down because many vampires like to turn people and have them be their playthings. Count Dracula was one of the worst offenders! He claimed he kept falling in love, but look where it got him. He already had three brides and he might still be with us today if he hadn't gone after that fourth.

You should never turn someone out of revenge or hate. This may be your idea of ultimate revenge, but do you really want a mortal enemy made into an immortal one? This is not a way to teach a lesson. It is worse if you do it out of some sick sense of humor, turning someone into something they hate. You are guaranteeing the vindictive vampires discussed above. Lucky for me, they will probably only come after you and leave the rest of us vampires alone.

TURNING PROCESS

There are as many stories floating around about how to be turned into a vampire as there are mythical cures for baldness. There is only one way to turn people into vampires and it won't be accidental. You must drink their blood and almost bring them to the point of death. They then have to feed on vampire blood in the same amount that was taken from them. You will have to help them drink your blood by placing their mouth directly on top of a bleeding wound you have created and hold them there until they have finished. This may sound easy, but as they drain you of your blood you will become very weak and their head will feel as if it were filled with lead weights. I suggest lying down so that you don't have to hold their head in place so much as cradle it. Having what seems like a large amount of blood drained from you will not kill you. Blood loss is not fatal to vampires, but it will make you weak and, if drained completely, will turn you into a savage beast. It is a good idea to have a source of blood around so that you can feed after this process. You will need to do this if you wish to recover before you rest at sunrise. You can have some blood for your spawn ready if you want to be nice, but it is not necessary since they have already fed off you. They will have no memory of being turned. Their last memory will be of you beginning to drink their blood. This permanent memory gap will last until a couple of hours after they have finished drinking your blood. They will be awake for those hours, but a little loopy, and then proceed to pass out for a few short minutes at the end. Be prepared for those few hours of wakefulness. They will have a strong craving for blood and will eat ravenously if presented with blood while in this state. Treat them as a baby who is nursing. If you have brought them food, gently guide them to and away from it so they do not drink too much. When they awaken, you will have a full vampire with original human personality intact (assuming you took my advice and didn't scar them emotionally), and they will remember their actions from here on out. They will be disoriented for a short time and will have a craving for something. It will take them a while to figure out that craving is for blood.

TURNING MYTHS

It is important that you only drink enough blood to bring them close to death. Many legends out there say that a mortal must be completely drained of blood to turn. This is false, and will kill them. Many vampires have accidentally killed loved ones because of this misconception. Then they end up destroying themselves out of grief. This is like the vampire equivalent of the Darwin Awards. The whole rumor makes no sense! How is the person you are attempting to turn going to drink blood if they are dead? Vampires who

believe this don't deserve immortality.

While these misconceptions may sound foolish, they are important to understand. You should have a full understanding of the turning process, as well as our history. The most common rumor is that a person can be turned by a single bite. It's not true—no way, no how. Thank goodness too, because if it were true, then vampires would soon outnumber humans, and the world would look a lot more like *Daybreakers*! While incomprehensible, I mention this myth first because it has the most widespread background and could lead to serious repercussions. Before mass media spread images so rapidly, we vampires were not forced to keep our actions so discreet. During these olden times, many vampires would turn mortals against their will and leave them on the street. This would often give the appearance of the dead coming back as vampires. As you may have guessed, these abandoned vampires had a low survival rate and were quickly butchered by the mob-like locals. Rather than leave them to this fate, it would be kinder to drain them completely.

I'm not suggesting you kill everyone, but there are guidelines to follow. It is recommended to spread out your feeding from individuals. I would never feed from the same person more than once every two weeks. You see, people who have addictive personalities, suffer from depression, or are lonely can get hooked on the euphoric chemicals released when we feed. This addiction and intense craving can actually have disturbing side effects. The most common and obvious is that they become infatuated with you. They are constantly offering you their blood to get their high. This in itself is more annoying than dangerous, but this need for your feeding on them can lead to the loss of their critical thinking. Much like a junkie loses sight of everything around them beyond getting their next fix, this impaired state of mind makes them more likely to share your secret. A less common side effect is that they start thinking of themselves as some kind of vampire hybrid and try to feed from blood hoping that it will give them that feeling of euphoria. Luckily, today all it does is get them thrown in jail. Back in the day, if mobs saw someone feeding on another person, that person would have their head ripped off and set on fire, no questions asked.

Ancient Slavic and Romanian cultures believed someone could be born a vampire. Back then it wasn't because we were being blamed for knocking up women, but through not understanding medical science and being overly superstitious. If babies were born with certain birth defects, specific birthmarks, born with teeth, or any other number of abnormalities, then they were believed to be vampires. Sometimes the kid was just out of luck before they were even born. They might have been cursed in the womb. If a child was the seventh born after the mother previously had six of the same gender, then you were said to be a vampire. I think all those youngest siblings out there can be thankful they were just treated like the baby all their lives. Being treated like a vampire is a lot more painful. Also, if a child was born or conceived between Christmas and Epiphany (the celebration of the Magi visiting the baby Jesus on January 6), then you had a reason to complain about your birthday falling on a holiday because yet again you would have been thought of as a vampire and treated as such. Still want to complain about getting stiffed on presents? If you had an illegitimate child and were an illegitimate child yourself, then chances are that you would be said to be giving birth to a vampire. They really put on the pressure to stay sexually pure back then. After a baby was declared a vampire, he or she would be disposed of in a typical gruesome fashion that only a human could come up with.

Even today, a common misconception is that if you drink from or turn pregnant women, their baby will be a vampire or daywalker. Nope, not true. Those babies will be born as normal humans. However, if you did turn a mother during pregnancy, the child will most likely grow up with a huge Freudian oral fixation. I can't explain it. It just happens. My best advice is to generally steer clear of expectant mothers. You don't want to be stuck with any therapy bills.

People were also thought to become vampires by sinning. Granted, we vampires can take some of the blame for this, since we often force our familiars into committing questionable acts before turning them. For the most part, this was used as a way to test their resolve of becoming a vampire. It was also used as entertainment, to see these silly humans break their own laws. Similar to the hazing process of college fraternities, except brought to the extreme. Committing violent crimes, practicing black magic, or dying unbaptized will not turn someone into a vampire. These beliefs really did more harm than good. There was nothing stopping us vampires from acting out our desires. We were already damned by just being undead, why not enjoy ourselves? Maybe if people were a little more accepting, we would not have had so many destructive tendencies. Think about that, human race.

Many cultures used to think specific causes of death could be enough to turn someone. Some of the ones I found most ridiculous were dying in childbirth, death by suicide, being murdered, and passing away between Christmas and Epiphany. December 25 through January 6 was an unlucky time of year. Friday the 13 is not looking so bad anymore, right? There was also a belief that if an animal killed a person, they could come back as a vampire. This is nonsense, but considering the fact that when someone survives a werewolf bite they turn into one, I understand where it comes from.

Only humans can be turned into vampires. You

can't turn your Pomeranian puppy into a lifelong companion. There will be no legion of vampire bunnies that drain the juice from a farmer's vegetable patch. Even werewolves that are part human cannot be turned into some kind of super crossbreed that will be the most powerful creature on earth. A human must be 100 percent *Homo sapiens*, if they are to be turned. Even the close primate relatives like chimpanzees, gorillas, and orangutans are not eligible for vampire life.

The most recent and hilarious belief is that vampires are aliens from outer space. Although I do not know where we vampires originated from, I can almost guarantee we are not these Space Vampires be-

coming more popular in media. I also doubt our home world would be called Drakulon or some other ridiculous wordplay from popular literature. This is a sci-fi/fantasy marketing dream that sells products, but has no base in historical accuracy. If we were an advanced species from outer space, I guarantee we would not have come to a planet that spends half the time in sunlight before developing something to shield us from its deadly rays. This one just doesn't make sense!

Now that you know how to turn someone (and how someone cannot be turned), remember to choose your prey wisely. I don't care if you spread the crazy rumors or not, just don't believe in them yourself.

— XIV —

Eternity: That's a Long Time

L iving indefinitely may sound wonderful to a short-lived human, but the reality of it can be extremely boring. The first few decades are the honeymoon period. You are discovering and fine-tuning your newly acquired powers, and feeling like a god among mortals. However, these times fade and soon it will feel as if you are an isolated island in the middle of an unfamiliar ocean of strangers. As the people you know begin to die, the places you know are built over, and the things you took as normal begin to change, the weight of time begins to press down on you. Sure, going from horse to airplane travel is wonderful, but such drastic changes to your original way of life can be traumatic. It is important for vampires to find things to keep them occupied and entertained or else they go mad. If this issue is not addressed, then destructive behavior follows and that can eventually lead to your downfall. Trust me, it has happened to the best vampires. Don't let it happen to you!

KILLING TIME

Most vampires are extremely well read and educated. Books are an easy way to pass the time, which is why so many vampires have extensive libraries that would impress any scholar. However, books can only fill so much time. It is a good idea to keep up on the latest technological advances. You don't want to look like you're in your twenties and act like an old geezer, so I suggest you learn about the latest gadgets and scientific mediums. If you insist on remaining a Luddite, at least read more than trashy novels. Sure, they are fun and sometimes you will pick up a no-brainer humor book (perhaps even a survival guide) that is a true masterpiece that flawlessly blends information with the comedic wit of true genius, but those are hard to come by. Books like this survival guide, I mean genius books that stand the test of time, only come along once a decade or so. Make sure to read books of substance. This will give you good conversation pieces and hopefully teach an old dog some new tricks.

I am of the belief that you can never learn too many skills. Some might be practical, like weapons training to help you survive. Others might be less useful but more impressive, like juggling or making balloon animals. The important thing is that you enjoy your chosen skill. If you don't like dancing, then don't take classes. Without the passion of flamenco you cannot foxtrot with the best.

Don't dismiss things right away either. You might be surprised at some hidden enjoyments you never expected. Cooking is a wonderful example that took me over a hundred years to discover. You may not be able to digest your food, but you can still taste it on your sensitive tongue and entertain potential meals/guests with your fine culinary skills. Please do not give up if a skill seems challenging—you will have a lifetime to master it. Just because you are a supernatural being does not mean you are going to instantly master a craft. Yes, your superior strength and experience will make you a quick learner, but like everything else, practice makes perfect. You can't instantly download kung fu into your brain to become a master.

Vampire Blood Sausage

INGREDIENTS	DIRECTIONS
2 lbs Pork Belly	1. Finely dice the pork belly.
3 lbs Human Blood	2. Mix the diced pork belly and blood by hand.
I prefer B+ blood	• Do not lick fingers clean till meat and blood are completely blended. Many vampires tend to overindulge like children with the cookie batter.
1 tsp Black Pepper	
1 tsp Nutmeg	
1 tsp Thyme	3. Mix in all your pepper, nutmeg, thyme and red onions.
¼ cup Pine Nuts	
1 cup Red Onions (Thinly Sliced)	4. Pour mixture into 38/40 hog casing.
	5. Poach for 25 minutes.
	6. Fry in pan prior to serving.

Hobbies are always a fun way to pass eternity. You might wish to collect some strange and unusual items. Building models, if done correctly, can eat up lots of time. I did ships in a bottle for a while, but lost too many to throwing them against the wall in frustration, which brings me to my next pearl of wisdom—I would suggest your hobbies be relaxing and not an agitation. With immense strength can come immense repair bills.

Creative endeavors can also be an enriching way to spend your immortal life. They are based on your imagination, and there is no limit to the amount of time you can spend on the process. Come to think of it, that's probably why I am writing this book. We vampires make the best authors (but I'm sure you already figured that out). With our years of vast knowledge and an ability to use a pseudonym to keep our true identity hidden, we can continue to write for years. Have you ever wondered why so many authors are recluses? Writing could be an excellent vampire career or creative outlet.

Other artistic pursuits that you can enjoy but avoid as a career choice would be painting (since we all know paintings are never worth anything until the artist is declared legally dead) or the performing arts, which put your face in the public eye. Being a rock star is not the best choice, despite what some books might suggest. Without going into a lot of detail, have you ever wondered why Janis Joplin, Amy Winehouse, Jimmy Hendrix, Kurt Cobain, Jim Morrison, and so many other musicians have passed away at the ripe young age of twenty-seven? I just wish Elvis would stop popping up all over the place.

Being a world traveler will keep you busy for several human lifetimes. I am not just talking about weeklong vacations to tourist traps. Truly immerse yourself into different cultures of the world. Learn new languages and traditions. Live among (and eat) new types of people. Civilizations developed their unique cultures over centuries, and it will take you at least a couple of years to truly learn about each one for yourself.

SLEEP THE DAYS AWAY

If you become completely bored out of your mind, there is another option. You know when the walls of despair start creeping in and nothing in life seems to satisfy you anymore? Well, then it might be time to take a long, overdue hibernation. Sleep for a solid fifty to a hundred years, and chances are you will awaken to a whole new world. This should not be done lightly. There are many dangers you will encounter, and if the proper steps are not taken, you may find yourself never arising again.

First and foremost, make sure the area you choose has no probability of disturbance. Think fast, where do you think this could be? Trick question: No place can be completely safe! This is a time when you will be forced to think much bigger than yourself. Like almost all real estate choices, location, location, location will be of the utmost importance. Unlike human homebuyers, you are not worried about trivial things such as resale value. You want to make sure that the location you're in will be around when you wake up. You will want to choose places with stable governments. Rome wasn't built in a day, and it didn't fall in a day either. After a string of bad emperors, as soon as they created two capitals (one in Rome and the other in Constantinople), I was out of there. Over time, if you follow world affairs, you too will be able to easily foresee these events. History does tend to repeat itself. You will also want to choose locations that have a low probability of completely destroying the structure you are in. Natural disasters are impossible to avoid, but some are easier to withstand than others. Try to avoid being on fault lines, in flood or fire areas, near tornado country, and next to active volcanoes. Oceanfront properties are great for active use, but never hibernate there. Tsunamis and hurricanes may be the large events that come to mind, but even the ocean air is corrosive and requires constant maintenance or else structures are eaten away. If you are not around to maintain and oversee these repairs, the effects could be deadly. Things like global warming and nuclear weapons have made finding a proper location more daunting than ever! It sounds stressful, but all these things must be considered in advance of hibernation if you are to have a safe and restful slumber.

The shelter itself is just as important as where you decide to rest. Don't limit yourself to the conventional thinking of a house. As we discussed in the chapter Home Is Where the Coffin Is, cemeteries offer some fantastic options from which to choose. For example, a mausoleum will offer protection from most destructive forces except earthquakes, volcanoes, and war. A coffin underground is safe from almost everything except grave robbers or, in some areas, flooding. Hurricane Katrina, in New Orleans, was a glaring example of how even being buried underground is not completely safe. Caves and tunnels are an excellent place to tuck away from civilization for a while, which is probably why they are the preferred hiding place of guerilla fighting groups. Just make sure there are no valuable mineral deposits surrounding you. Humans love to blow those places up and then pillage the resources. Dynamite is definitely an alarm clock you don't want waking you up.

Houses can work as well, but you will want to make sure they are well built, offer superior security, have excellent hiding and hibernation spots, and most importantly can be maintained financially for the duration of your rest. Inflation has caused more than one vampire's hiding spots to be exposed, mostly to sun courtesy of a wrecking ball, which is why vampire bodies have never been discovered in this manner.

WAKE UP AND SMELL THE BLOOD

Much like a bear must store fat for their long hibernation, so must you store items for your awakening.

Your immediate concern will be food. If you do not feed soon after waking from a long slumber, you will slip into a ravenous state. Depending on how long you are asleep, storing blood could have many logistical problems. The best option is to plan for your return by having food brought to you at a designated time. With vampire urging, many rituals have been developed for this purpose—or did you think that cultures tend to sacrifice beautiful scantily clad virgins by coincidence? This being said, you don't need human blood when you wake up; animals (literally, a sacrificial lamb) can provide you with the sustenance required.

Less pressing, but no less important, will be your need for clothing. We do not hibernate naked, but fashion changes quickly. After a decade or two, your clothes will be so out of date that you will just look downright crazy. Tights and a codpiece may have been the rage when you went to sleep in Elizabethan England, but today they will only draw stares. One way to avoid this is to wake on Halloween, Mardi Gras, or some other celebration that encourages costumes. You can also arrange for new clothes to be brought with your food. It is recommended that you eat before changing. Due to your hunger you may be messier than usual when consuming your food.

You will also need some cash on hand and at your disposal immediately. If you thought ahead, you will have a financial nest egg waiting upon your return. This is where modern currency can be a headache. Currency is constantly going out of use due to regime change or being updated to meet higher security standards. If you are away long enough, your currency may be useless or a valuable collector's item that will draw unwanted attention. This is where hoarding valuable minerals like diamonds or gold comes in handy. Currencies' values fluctuate, but raw materials often keep a strong relative value. Your hibernation shelter will do for the immediate living arrangements, so that is one relief, but for how long is completely up to you. Some stay there indefinitely, while others have nicer accommodations already waiting for their arrival.

After your basic needs of food, clothing, and shelter have been met, you must immediately study your new surroundings. Before you can go about the town, make sure you can blend in appropriately. It is not acceptable to be ignorant of large events such as landing on the moon or recent customs like *not* wearing a sword in public. Be wary of expressions that could lead to awkward conversations or unintentional insults. Not calling a woman fat may seem like common sense no matter what century you wake up in. Sadly for a young man who came upon a recently awakened female vampire by the name of Licinia, we learn about the complexity of human language. This young man was overcome by her beauty and called her "phat"—not realizing this meant "Pretty Hot and Tempting," she ripped him to shreds.

Hopefully you will enjoy your life as a vampire for ages to come. However, if you ever feel the walls of immortality closing in on you, I can only hope this chapter may save you from the wretched vampire epidemic, sunicide.

— XV —

The Laws of the Vampire: Follow Them or Else . . .

As with any intelligent species, there are rules that vampires must follow. We do not have many, but the few that we do have are imperative to our survival, and we don't have flexible punishments. Obey them or die. No eating cake here. Although we attempt to be fair and give you a trial by our elders . . . you're pretty much guilty until proven innocent in our courts. We prefer to err on the side of caution. Better to vote guilty if we are unsure than let a guilty party go free, only to break another rule. Since vampires are not found innocent very often, never push your luck.

Law I: *Thou shalt never reveal thy true nature to a mortal . . . and let that mortal live.*

Our existence must be kept a secret. This is the key to our survival, which is why it is rule number one. Yes, you can reveal yourself if you wish to play with your food for a bit, but you must kill or turn them when you are done and before they have any contact with another mortal. This rule excludes human servants, as they are  not considered actual people (more on that in law number four). The vampire falling in love with a human story is all Hollywood and literature. For some reason, girls eat up the whole eternal love with a tortured soul thing, but it doesn't fly in the real world.

Law II: *Thou shall not turn children, or those mortals unable to survive on their own, into vampires.*

This is cruel (even for us vampires) and creates a higher chance of us being revealed to the public. Every now and then a child is turned out of some leftover human longing to be a parent, but the error is quickly realized. While not part of this rule, now is a good time to reiterate how much I discourage turning teenagers. I know they can survive on their own, but there is nothing more annoying than a vampire trapped in constant teenage angst. Do everyone a favor and stick to turning adults like a good vampire should.

Law III: *Thou shalt not kill another vampire, unless required to do so through self-defense or enforcing our laws.*

Let's be honest, this rule is rarely enforced. You might be asked about it, but unless you are stupid enough to do it in front of a possible witness, any excuse will be accepted. I think this one was thrown in just to make us feel warm and fuzzy about our peers.

Law IV: *Thou shalt not kill a vampire's human servant.*

Human servants are the only mortals allowed to know about our existence, because they are considered extensions of their vampire masters and not individuals. A true servant would be under their master's control. This rule is not enforced by an elder vampire, but by the servant's master, which means things can get ugly fast. Unless you want to pick a fight, obey this law. Alternatively, if you do want to pick a fight, it is a great way to get around law number three, since you can now claim self-defense. Just be careful to kill their servant by "accident." I'll give you the defense for free this time: "That was your servant? Sorry, I thought it was a meal o' gram. My bad."

Law V: *Thou shalt not create other vampires for wars or disputes.*

It is important for us to keep our numbers down. Too many vampires would greatly increase the chances of us being discovered, and deplete our food sources. Vampires cannot afford to take a short-term view with such unnaturally long lives. We cannot afford the limited thinking of humans. Besides, imagine the resources needed to support an army of undead soldiers. The only time this law was lifted was during our war with the Lycans, and even then it was highly debated. However, due to the enormous casualty rates of the war, it was ultimately deemed essential for our survival and victory.

Law VI: *The secrets of the vampire must be guarded at all cost.*

This one is pretty self-explanatory. Keep your mouth shut, and if you discover any leaks, dispose of the problem immediately. There is no such thing as an innocent bystander here. If you are found to have not done everything in your power to keep the secret buried, then you will be dealt with as well.

Law VII: *A coven may create their own rules and laws so long as they do not conflict with the existing Supreme Vampire Laws.*

These laws vary vastly, so make sure you are aware of all laws before becoming part of a covenant. A lot of them will make sense based on the time period and location in which you are living, but every now and then one shows up that will baffle the mind and could lead to some unwanted sentencing. I have included some of the more amusing ones below.

1) *It is illegal to whiten fangs through a dentist or any other oral hygiene product.*
2) *Vampires may not speak in a baby voice when addressing another vampire's familiar.*

RULES OR GUIDELINES

There are a few Supreme Vampire Laws that have been revoked over time or were only enforced for a short period. Some of these may still be active in isolated Covenants, so it's probably a good idea to be familiar with them. Since they are no longer laws, we shall call them rules.

Rule I: *Thou shalt only turn mortals of beautiful appearance into vampires.*

This law was originally enacted during our satanic period, when we thought of ourselves as demons and agents of the devil. The theory was that turning beautiful people insulted God by taking them away from him. This feeling of working for the devil came out of a deep self-loathing. We were dealing with our inability to die naturally and our strong religious upbringing while we were human, which is where a lot of the terminology, such as referring to our powers as "the dark gifts," originated. We really hated ourselves. The whole beautiful people thing was all about our egos and wanting to be surrounded by hotties. You spend eternity looking at someone, you better enjoy doing it, am I right?

Rule II: *Vampires shall not associate with Lycans.*

This was a short-lived law occurring during the great Vampire-Lycan War. It was a bloodbath and both sides suffered terrible casualties. By the end of it, our numbers were decimated. The only true winners were the humans. If you wish to learn more about it, you will have to look somewhere else. This is a survival guide, not a history book.

EPILOGUE:
EULOGY

Heed my warning and buy a copy of this book for all the vampires you know. If you are going to turn someone, at least leave a copy of this book behind. No one should become a vampire and be left to his or her own survival devices. It's just cruel! Plus, the more copies of this book I sell, the longer it will be before I am forced to get another job. Help support my desire not to have to work again for a very long, long time . . . perhaps even eternity.

ACKNOWLEDGMENTS

Thank you

To my sister, who was my first editor and made me appear literate. (Is this sentence grammatically correct?)

To my wife and children, for your constant love and support. (Especially when I switch into crazy artist mode.)

To my parents, for always encouraging my creativity growing up. (Even when that included turning our backyard into the lost city of Atlantis.)

To Stephen, for always supporting my artistic endeavors and being ready to lend a helping hand. (Even when that meant flooding the backyard to create Atlantis.)

To Mark and Andrew, for guiding me through the process of having my first book professionally published.

Printed in the United States
by Baker & Taylor Publisher Services